Researching Primary Education: Methods and Issues

This book increases understanding of, and provides inspiration for, the conduct of research in primary/elementary education. The contributing authors discuss and evaluate the selection and development of research methods used for their own innovatory projects. They explore the relationship between their choice of research methods, the frameworks for analysis used and research findings. In so doing they address the topical and controversial issues posed by these methods and alternative data-gathering techniques. These include:

- the case for the use of random-controlled trials to inform policy-making and improve classroom practice;
- the benefits of combining quantitative psychometric and sociometric data and qualitative interview data in a 'mixed methods' approach;
- the relationship between research and teacher development;
- conducting document analysis to examine the portrayal of teachers and education in the regional and national news;
- children as researchers researching their peers; and
- the contribution of qualitative research in cross-national projects.

In research on teaching and learning in primary schools, accessing the views and experiences of children is crucial. Consequently, the possibilities and limitations of data collection techniques for collecting the views of children and concerns about validity and ethics posed by the power relationships between researchers and research participants are central concerns for the book.

This book is based on a special issue of *Education 3-13 International Journal of Primary, Elementary and Early years Education.*

Rosemary Webb has had a varied career in primary education as a teacher, a professional officer at the National Curriculum Council, lecturer and researcher and became a Professor in the School of Education at the University of Manchester in 2006. She is a past Chair of the Association for the Study of Primary Education (ASPE) and was convenor of the British Educational Research Association/ ASPE Special Interest Group on primary education. She has researched and published widely on primary education and on qualitative research.

Researching Primary Education: Methods and Issues

Edited by Rosemary Webb

Routledge
Taylor & Francis Group
LONDON AND NEW YORK

First published 2010 by Routledge
2 Park Square, Milton Park, Abingdon, Oxon, OX14 4RN

Simultaneously published in the USA and Canada
by Routledge
711 Third Avenue, New York, NY 10017

Routledge is an imprint of the Taylor & Francis Group, an informa business

First issued in paperback 2012

This book is a reproduction of *Education 3-13*, vol. 37, issue 4. The Publisher requests to those authors who may be citing this book to state, also, the bibliographical details of the special issue on which the book was based

Typeset in Times by Value Chain, India

British Library Cataloguing in Publication Data
A catalogue record for this book is available from the British Library

ISBN13: 978-0-415-56752-7 (hbk)
ISBN13: 978-0-415-63383-3 (pbk)

CONTENTS

Introduction

Researching primary education: methods and issues

The last decade has witnessed major challenges to previous orthodoxies of educational research, stimulating new approaches to the collection, analysis and validation of data and fuelling controversy amongst both educational researchers and policy-makers. The seeds for such changes in the British context go back to the late-1990s spate of much publicised critiques of the state of educational research in the UK (Hargreaves 1996; Hillage et al. 1998; Tooley with Darby 1998). It was argued that a combination of poor research design and execution, coupled with partisan biases from researchers, frequently led to unwarranted conclusions that were of no practical use to policy-makers. A contrast was drawn with medical research which, unlike educational research, was viewed as having the benefits of developing cumulative knowledge as to 'what works' which could then inform the everyday practice of medical practitioners. Part of the problem, it was suggested, lay with the preponderance of small-scale qualitative research studies whose small unrepresentative samples meant that no wider generalisations from the research were possible. Continuing critics of the quality of British educational research, such as Gorard, have pointed to the 'generally low level of numeric competence in UK educational research' (2002b, 236) and have advocated the greater use of numeric secondary data analysis (see also Smith 2008).

Such criticisms of mainstream educational research in the UK have been associated with the growing influence of research traditions focussing on 'what works' or what is 'effective' in education in order to inform 'evidence-based' policy formation (Davies 1999). The use of randomised controlled trials (RCTs) has been promoted by some educational researchers (e.g. Fitz-Gibbon 1999), some social scientists (e.g. Oakley 2000) and some evaluators (e.g. Boruch 1997) as the key feature of the use of evidence-based research to inform policy making. Indeed, Fitz-Gibbon actually takes the term 'evidence-based' to refer to 'information arising from experimental methods' (1999, 33). Allied with this has been the advocacy for educational research of the systematic review methodology that had already been developed in the medical field with the Cochrane Collaboration (Torgerson 2003). Thus, in 2000, the Department for Education and Skills funded the Evidence for Policy and Practice Information and Coordinating (EPPI) Centre at the University of London Institute of Education to support a programme of systematic reviews of educational research (Oakley 2002). The methodological criteria used in evaluating the validity of studies incorporated in a systematic review gave the highest credibility to studies based on the measurement of variables and where there were explicit and replicable procedures of physical or statistical control, with the RCT viewed as the gold standard.

Two recent developments mark the growing influence in British educational research of approaches that hitherto had been restricted (unlike in the United States) to medical research. The first was the establishment of the Institute for Effective Education at the University of York in 2007 – a research centre explicitly devoted to the promotion of evidence-based policies in education and directed by Robert Slavin, a prominent American educational psychologist whose advocacy of RCTs and systematic reviews is well known (see e.g. Slavin 2008). The second is the establishment in 2009 of a new journal *Effective Education*, edited by Paul Connolly at Queen's University in Belfast, devoted to papers addressing the effectiveness of educational programmes through experimental empirical studies, secondary analyses or meta analyses of large datasets, or systematic reviews. Carole Torgerson's work has been influential in the design and execution of RCTs in Britain and her contribution in this collection provides a very useful overview of their rationale, together with illustrations of how they have been used in research on primary schooling.

Such a privileging of quantitative experimental methodology in 'what counts as valid educational research' has provoked, not surprisingly perhaps, some forceful critiques of systematic reviews from scholars whose work has been associated with qualitative research methodology (e.g. Hammersley 2001; MacLure 2005; Vulliamy 2004). Criticisms relate both to the procedures of systematic reviewing, which Hammersley argues are based on outmoded 'positivist' principles which erroneously suggest that the scientific method can operate on the basis of fully explicit procedures, and to the privileging of experimental methodology. The latter, it is argued, fails to address the unanticipated and unintended outcomes of innovation and neglects local context and process/implementation issues and consequent problems of innovation transfer. While such criticisms of experimental methodology are often portrayed as a product of a quantitative/qualitative divide in educational research, Vulliamy (2004) argues that this is a misnomer in that the divide has always been one of epistemological and ontological prior assumptions (often referred to as 'paradigms' in the literature) rather than the use of quantitative or qualitative data *per se*. To illustrate this, he draws upon the work of Byrne (2002) – a quantitative researcher who adopts an ontology of 'complex realism' and who uses computer-based neural net, simulation and modelling techniques to interpret the nature of complex social systems and their trajectories but who makes similar criticisms of RCTs as qualitative researchers.

A recognition of this epistemological/ontological divide also provides a useful backcloth for the currently fashionable advocacy of 'mixed methods' or 'multi-method' approaches to educational research. Gorard and Taylor (2004) suggest that the fact that there is 'so little education research that routinely combines numeric and other evidence' (7) can be blamed on unnecessary paradigm wars. Gorard's view (2002a, 2004) is that we should move beyond the paradigm debate and use whatever methods, or blend of methods, suits the research problem at hand. This is a seemingly attractive position, especially for policy-makers who understandably are impatient with philosophical discourse. However, it raises controversial questions as to the role of theory in educational research (Nash 2004), just as a similar argument thirty years ago that the distinctions between research methodology paradigms are overdrawn and artificial (Reichardt and Cook 1979) proved equally controversial (Patton 1988; Guba and Lincoln 1988). While the issues surrounding multi-method research have a long history of debate, a positive outcome of the current emphasis on mixing methods has been the broadening of approaches beyond the more traditional combination of questionnaire and interview data. The contribution by Elias

Avramidis and Alison Wilde in this collection is a good example of such broadening, with its innovative combination of quantitative psychometric and sociometric data and qualitative interview data. In research in education a range of documents are usually drawn upon to portray the national, local and/or school context. They are also often used to compare intended policy and actual practice and so examine the gap between rhetoric and reality. Anders Hansen's study is unusual in its exclusive focus on document analysis as he takes us through the process of examining the representation of teachers in the national and local press.

Since the United Nations Convention on the Rights of the Child (1989) promoted the rights of children to be involved in all matters concerning them there has been an increasing interest in the 'pupil voice' in education. However, the development of ways of accessing the 'pupil voice' is still in its infancy in many primary schools. Schools are constrained by the power differentials between teachers and pupils, the differing importance attached to issues of concern for teachers and pupils, the inequality between pupils caused by a reliance on speaking and listening skills and the degree to which tradition and government prescription renders the curriculum and many aspects of school life seemingly non-negotiable. Nevertheless there is a steady growth in research into pupils' views on all aspects of education (see, for example, Volume 36 of *Education 3–13*) which reveals the potential for transforming teaching and learning and strengthening teacher-pupil relationships of listening to pupils and of taking their views into account in making decisions about classroom practice and school policies. Such research, together with a commitment to finding ways to improve pupil learning, the personalisation of that learning in the Primary National Strategy (PNS) and the survey of pupil views included in Ofsted inspections, combine to encourage and assist schools to find out more about what pupils think of their school experiences.

In acknowledgement of the importance of accessing and acting on pupil perspectives in researching primary education, there are three contributions on this theme. Oral data collected through interviews and discussions, individually and in groups, play a central part in collecting pupils' views. However, as recognised by Jill Porter such data are fraught with problems of communication and bias, especially in accessing the perspectives of children with learning difficulties. Caroline Lodge contrasts the use of visual images in the media with the unduly cautious approach to such material by researchers which serves to deny children alternatives to text as a means to express their views. While recognising the vital considerations of ethics and safety, she argues for research to adopt a wider and more innovative approach to the collection of visual data in order to increase the research participation of children and young people. Elisabeth Barratt Hacking and Robert Barratt describe a project on children's experiences of their local environment which sought to promote children's equal involvement with adults in the research process – designing and conducting research which collected both oral and visual data, tackling data analysis and disseminating their findings.

An unfortunate unintended consequence of the recent Research Assessment Exercise (RAE) across higher education institutions in the UK, the results of which determine future research funding, has been to discourage researchers from carrying out teacher development projects and from writing materials specifically for teachers in order to concentrate on publishing in high status academic journals. However, the rationale for much research in education to which most researchers are committed is to inform teachers' understanding of their pupils and to improve the quality of teaching and learning in schools. Martin Braund provides valuable insights into a development project to improve the quality of pupils' discussions in science and shows how the project data fed directly into training materials.

This special edition discusses a range of methods and addresses some key issues encountered in researching primary education. While it is acknowledged that these are shared by research in other phases of education, it is hoped that consideration of how they have been addressed in the primary school context will be of particular interest and assistance both to researchers, teachers and others carrying out research and to research users. The final contribution by Graham Vulliamy and Rosemary Webb describes the methodology of joint qualitative research projects on the impact of government reform on primary schooling conducted by English and Finnish researchers. As increasingly policymakers are borrowing ideas from the education systems of other countries in a bid to produce a better educated and more economically competitive workforce, researchers seek to analyse, compare and evaluate the impact of these ideas. The trend towards more comparative research and cross-national research projects is a crucially important one in our globalised world and one which is likely to be increasingly reflected in future editions of *Education 3–13*.

References

Boruch, R.F. 1997. *Randomized experiments for planning and evaluation.* London: Sage.

Byrne, D. 2002. *Interpreting quantitative data.* London: Sage.

Davies, P. 1999. What is evidence-based education? *British Journal of Educational Studies* 47, no. 2: 108–21.

Fitz-Gibbon, C.T. 1999. Education: High potential not yet realised. *Public Money and Management*, January-March: 33–40.

Gorard, S. 2002a. Can we overcome the methodological schism? Four models for combining qualitative and quantitative evidence. *Research Papers in Education* 17, no. 4: 345–61.

Gorard, S. 2002b. The role of secondary data in combining methodological approaches. *Educational Review* 54, no. 3: 231–37.

Gorard, S. 2004. Sceptical or clerical? Theory as a barrier to the combination of research methods. *Journal of Educational Enquiry* 5, no. 1: 1–21.

Gorard, S., and C. Taylor. 2004. *Combining methods in educational and social research.* London: Open University Press.

Guba, E.G., and Y.S. Lincoln. 1988. Do inquiry paradigms imply inquiry methodologies?. In *Qualitative approaches to evaluation in education: The silent scientific revolution*, ed. D.M. Fetterman. New York: Praeger.

Hammersley, M. 2001. On 'systematic' reviews of research literatures: A 'narrative' response to Evans and Benefield. *British Educational Research Journal* 27, no. 5: 543–54.

Hargreaves, D. 1996. Teaching as a research-based profession: Possibilities and prospects. *Teacher training agency annual lecture 1996.* London: Teacher Training Agency.

Hillage, J., R. Pearson, A. Anderson, and P. Tamkin. 1998. *Excellence in research in schools.* London: Department for Education and Employment/Institute of Employment Studies.

MacLure, M. 2005. 'Clarity bordering on stupidity': Where's the quality in systematic review? *Journal of Education Policy* 20, no. 4: 393–416.

Nash, R. 2004. Science as a theoretical practice: A response to Gorard from a sceptical cleric. *Journal of Educational Enquiry* 5, no. 2: 1–18.

Oakley, A. 2000. *Experiments in knowing: Gender and method in the social sciences.* Cambridge: Polity Press.

Oakley, A. 2002. Social science and evidence-based everything: The case of education. *Educational Review* 54, no. 3: 277–86.

Patton, M.Q. 1988. Paradigms and pragmatism. In *Qualitative approaches to evaluation in education: The silent scientific revolution*, ed. D.M. Fetterman. New York: Praeger.

Reichardt, C.S., and T.D. Cook. 1979. Beyond qualitative *versus* quantitative methods. In *Qualitative and quantitative methods in evaluation* research, ed. T.D. Cook and C.S. Reichardt, 7–32. Beverley Hills: Sage.

Slavin, R.E. 2008. Evidence-based reform in education: What will it take? *European Educational Research Journal* 7, no. 1: 124–28.

Smith, E. 2008. *Using secondary data in educational and social research.* Berkshire: Open University Press.

Tooley, J., with D. Darby. 1998. *Educational research – A critique.* London: Office for Standards in Education.

Torgerson, C.J. 2003. *Systematic reviewing.* London: Continuum.

Vulliamy, G. 2004. The impact of globalisation on qualitative research in comparative and international education. *Compare* 34, no. 3: 261–84.

Rosemary Webb

School of Education, University of Manchester, UK

Randomised controlled trials in education research: a case study of an individually randomised pragmatic trial

Carole J. Torgerson

Institute for Effective Education, University of York, UK

The randomised controlled trial (RCT) is an evaluative method used by social scientists in order to establish whether or not an intervention is effective. This contribution discusses the fundamental aspects of good RCT design. These are illustrated through the use of a recently completed RCT which evaluated an information and communication technology (ICT) intervention designed to improve the literacy (reading and spelling) abilities of 11- and 12-year-old children. Some of the limitations of this trial are discussed and suggestions outlined for how it could have been improved. It is demonstrated that it is possible to evaluate a widely-used intervention in a rigorous fashion and to obtain educationally meaningful results, which are of interest to the practitioner, policy maker and researcher.

Introduction

Recently, there has been a greater international awareness among policy makers, funders and practitioners of the need for researchers to establish, in an unbiased way, whether or not educational interventions (teaching programmes and practices, strategies and methods) are actually effective in improving children's educational outcomes. Stakeholders (policy-makers and practitioners) need to know *what would have happened* to children had they *not* been exposed to an intervention. Put another way, the counterfactual has to be revealed in relation to any improvement observed in children exposed to an intervention. To do this requires experimental research which uses a control group design. Whilst the US, for example, has a history of some educational researchers undertaking experimental research, this has until recently been largely confined to the field of educational psychology. In the last five years, however, policy makers and funders of educational research, particularly in the US but also in the UK and Ireland, are increasingly acknowledging that they need to seek and use results from experimental research to inform decision making at all levels.

Control groups can be formed in many ways, for example by 'matching' individual children or groups of children and then allocating one group to a treatment condition and one group to a control condition. Forming intervention and control groups through random allocation ensures that the groups are balanced in known and unknown characteristics at the start of the experiment. This article attempts to illustrate why the randomised controlled trial is the best method that all the aforementioned stakeholders can rely on when they need an answer to a 'what works?' question in education.

RCT is an evaluative method of elegant design used by social scientists in order to establish whether or not an intervention (programme, practice or strategy) is effective (Cook and Campbell 1979; Torgerson and Torgerson 2001; Torgerson and Torgerson 2008). Also known as 'true' experiments, RCTs have a simple design: two or more groups are formed by the random (or chance) allocation of individuals or clusters (classes, schools) of individuals. This method of allocation ensures that the two or more groups thus formed are equivalent at baseline on all known and unknown variables (with the exception of chance) that could affect outcome (for example, gender, socio-economic status, performance on a reading measure etc.). The groups are then either exposed to an intervention or to a control or comparison condition, which can either be an alternative intervention or no treatment control (normal classroom practice).

When a randomised controlled trial has been well-designed and well-conducted, and if the groups assembled through randomisation are sufficiently large, any differences in outcome observed between the groups at post-test can be ascribed to the intervention, rather than to some other known or unknown variable. The RCT is particularly well-suited to areas where there is considerable complexity in terms of causal pathways and mechanisms of action. Where a causal relationship is straightforward, such as a strong blow to the arm causing injury, then a RCT is not necessary to illuminate whether or not the action lead to the predicted outcome. In contrast, where the causal pathway and mechanism of action are more complex, such as training teachers to deliver a phonics-based reading programme causing improvement in children's literacy outcomes, then a RCT is *the* robust method to use in order to establish this causal relationship.

Medical researchers have long recognised that even a 'simple' drug trial may be in fact evaluating an incredibly complex intervention. For a drug to work it has to be taken in an effective dose; individuals comply differently; the chemical entity is absorbed through the gut at differential rates; once in the blood stream the drug has to reach the tissues on which it is to act; and genetic differences ensure that it works slightly differently between individuals. The RCT is the most rigorous research method able to deal adequately with such levels of complexity, inherent in the field of medical and social sciences in general, and the field of education in particular (Sheldon and Oakley 2002; Shadish, Cook, and Campbell 2002; Torgerson and Torgerson 2008). This is because, in principle, the design controls for *all* the alternative explanations for any difference in measured outcome.

Well-designed RCTs can contribute to a wide spectrum of knowledge. For example, they can demonstrate the effectiveness, or otherwise, of an educational policy; if sufficiently large, they can also look at differential effects in terms of participant characteristics, intervention implementation and fidelity, different measures of outcome etc. They can establish whether a theoretically-based intervention responds according to what the theory has predicted. Finally, they can enable the evaluation of teaching and learning practices to be undertaken in a robust fashion, by ruling out alternative explanations for observed improvements in measured outcomes by enabling a causal relationship between the intervention and outcome to be inferred.

The earliest RCTs in education

Some of the earliest RCTs using human subjects in the twentieth century were undertaken in the field of education, but they are currently not widely used in this field, particularly in the UK.

The history of the RCT design can be traced back to the 1920s and 30s when RA Fisher, a statistician, formalised random allocation within experimental agriculture (Fisher 1971). Later, in the 1940s, Lindquist (1940) adapted Fisher's texts on agricultural statistics and in doing so made some important methodological changes relevant to educational research. For Fisher the unit of analysis was a block of land, whereas Lindquist observed that the natural unit of observation for educational researchers was either the class or the school. Lindquist developed statistical methodology that was able to cope with the issue of children within the same class or the same school being more similar, in terms of their educational outcomes, to each other compared with children who in different classes or schools. Lindquist recognised that applying randomisation to human participants was different from applying it to crops, and many important methodological innovations in trial design since Fisher's time have been necessary in order to overcome the issue that human participants do not always do what the experimenter expects of them or wants them to do.

Controlled experiments in the field of literacy instruction for children with learning difficulties were conducted around the beginning of the twentieth century, although it is difficult to ascertain how the control groups in some of these studies were formed, and they may not have used true random allocation (Oakley 2000; Forsetlund, Chalmers, and Bjørndal 2007). According to Forsetlund, Chalmers, and Bjørndal (2007) the earliest studies that unequivocally used randomisation were published in the early 1930s. Two studies looked at the effect of counselling on students' performance (Walters 1931, 1932). In the first of these studies Walters (1931) described random allocation in an educational context: *'the 220 delinquent freshmen were divided into two groups by random sampling'* (Walters 1931). Walters noted that the *'delinquency in the counselled group had decreased 34 percent, while that of the control group had fallen only 13 percent, a net saving of 21 per cent'* (Walters 1931). In the second trial Walters (1932) described how 994 'freshman', or first year undergraduate students, were *'divided into three equal groups by random sampling'*. The aim of the study was to assess whether counselling students by older peers or tutors resulted in better progress than no counselling.

Application of the RCT methodology from agriculture to education is relatively simple compared with applying the method to a health care setting. In agriculture the sample, field area containing plants, is observed before randomisation and the land can be divided into equally sized blocks to ensure that field is evenly randomised to the two groups. In health care research, participants are usually recruited sequentially and it is not often possible to randomise the participants all at once. In education research the situation is more analogous to the situation in agricultural research. Usually we have known pupils nested within a known set of classes nested within a known set of schools. Consequently randomisation, as in agriculture, can be undertaken on the whole sample at one time. Children within schools are also relatively easier to keep within a trial, unlike patients who frequently do not re-attend appointments for post-test evaluations. Furthermore, assessing children on educational outcomes is routine for teachers, whereas health care professionals often do not use quantitative methods for assessing illness progression.

On the other hand, one problem that affects educational trials, unlike health care studies, is the issue of often there being a necessity to randomise by cluster or group. For most health care interventions it is possible to randomise at the level of the patient. For many educational interventions we need to randomise by class or school. This means that we need many more children in a cluster randomised trial compared with an individually randomised study. Statistical power for cluster trials is a function (mainly) of the number of clusters rather than of the number of children within a cluster. Consequently, it is better to have many small schools each with relatively few children than small numbers of large schools. Thus, trials among primary or elementary school children have the advantage relative to trials among children at secondary or high schools as the latter are larger and power will be relatively lower for a given number of children compared with trials in primary or elementary schools.

Whatever the type of trial we are proposing to undertake, it is crucial that the trial is reported well and is of high quality; otherwise parents, teachers, policy makers and researchers could be misled.

Characteristics of rigorous RCTs

Since Walter's pioneering trials from the 1930s, trials using human participants have developed and several key characteristics of a rigorous RCT can be described.

Preserving random allocation

Randomisation minimises selection bias if all the participants are randomly allocated and they are all retained within their allocated groups for analysis. People often change groups after allocation because of ethical, educational or administrative reasons. But in order to preserve the original random allocation they must be treated in the analysis as if they have retained membership of their *original* groups. This is known as 'intention-to-treat analysis' (ITT analysis).

Another recognised problem is failure to implement the random allocation successfully. For a variety of reasons, some researchers over-ride the random allocation and allocate participants into their groups on grounds of preference. This approach introduces selection bias and can render the results of the experiment invalid. To avoid this problem a rigorous trial uses third party allocation, whereby a researcher who has no vested interest (intellectual or financial) in the result of the trial, performs the allocation procedure. This is also known as 'concealed allocation'.

Other potential problems facing trials among human participants include lack of compliance and failure to produce post-test data. High attrition (drop-out) can introduce bias, especially if this is differential (i.e. more are lost to post-test in one group compared with the other). Statistical approaches for trying to deal with attrition have been developed, but none is entirely satisfactory. A rigorous trial, therefore, features low or no attrition after random allocation.

The preceding sections described how selection bias can be introduced at the randomisation point or afterwards. Even if a trial has been properly randomised and there is 100% post-test completion, bias can still be introduced if post-tests are marked by researchers who are not blind to the treatment allocation. Some post-test assessments (for example, holistic writing abilities) are susceptible to different interpretations, and these interpretations may be affected, either consciously or unconsciously, by the assessor having knowledge of the group allocation. Consequently it is important that post-test assessments are carried out by personnel who are blind to group membership.

CONSORT guidelines for reporting RCTs

Many, if not most, trials in any field do not report key methodological criteria to enable the reader to judge the quality of the trial. Clearly, evidence from a poor quality trial is less reliable than evidence from a high quality study. In the 1990s, this problem of poor reporting was so widespread in health care research that leading journal editors and trial methodologists developed the CONSORT statement for the reporting of medical trials (Altman 1996; Moher, Jones, and Lepage 2001). These guidelines were drawn up using methodological work as a basis, and are now widely accepted as a consensus 'gold' standard in the design of trials. The guidelines have been adopted by the American Psychological Association, and are beginning to be adopted in the field of education research (e.g. in the recently established UK-based education journal 'Effective Education': http://www.tandf.co.uk/journals/titles/19415532.asp). The guidelines include a number of items recommended as being essential to ensure methodological rigour, for example, whether the method of random allocation was described, whether the sample size was justified, whether the outcomes were assessed 'blind' to group allocation.

Originally the CONSORT statement was developed for the reporting of pharmacological trials. However, because the key issues of methodology described for pharmacological trials are very similar to other trials this means that, with slight modification, a variation of the statement has been developed for non-pharmacological trials and most of the quality items can readily be applied to educational trials (Boutron et al. 2008). In the following a description of an educational trial using CONSORT guidance is described.

An example of a RCT in a school setting

A recently completed RCT undertaken by the author and others, evaluated an information and communication technology (ICT) intervention designed to improve the literacy (reading and spelling) abilities of 11- and 12-year-old children (see Brooks et al. 2006 for the full report of this trial). The study aimed to assess whether the intervention using additional ICT support would help to improve the literacy (spelling and reading) attainment of Year seven pupils in a secondary school. The trial was explicitly designed to enable it to conform to the highest methodological standards as described in the CONSORT statement (see above). Consequently it is methodologically innovative (for an educational trial) in its design and reporting. Further, as far as we are aware, at the time of publication of the original report it was the largest UK-based individually randomised trial undertaken in field of literacy and ICT (n = 155); it is of significance for methodological debate and for practical decisions.

Randomisation of individual children in the school was employed to establish balanced treatment and control groups within the environment of real classrooms. Careful consideration was given to design in terms of sample size calculations, implementation features, data collection, and analysis in order to ensure a methodologically robust outcome.

Previous research in ICT and literacy

Ideally, before any trial is started a rigorous systematic review of the existing literature should be undertaken (Torgerson 2003). A systematic review can aid trial design in a number of ways. Firstly, it can establish whether or not another trial is actually needed and feasible to implement. Secondly, it can help to inform the design features of a trial, such as what plausible effect size it might be possible to detect. Torgerson and Elbourne (2002) undertook a systematic review of the effectiveness of ICT on spelling instruction and found only seven small trials, which were not large enough either singly or in combination to enable a policy decision to be made. When the trials were combined in a meta-analysis there was a trend towards a modest benefit of ICT, but this was not statistically significant. More recently, Torgerson and Zhu (2004) undertook a systematic review of the effectiveness of ICT on literacy instruction in general and found only two randomised trials evaluating the use of computer-aided instruction in reading. One of the trials found a non-statistically significant moderately positive effect size for reading, and the other found a non-statistically significant negative effect size.

No previous experimental research has evaluated this particular intervention. *Pre-experimental* research (i.e. research using a one group pre-post-test design with no control group) had been undertaken in a school with Year seven pupils during the school year 2003 4. The previous research identified a subgroup of children on the basis of performance on a single spelling test; they were then given the intervention followed by a post-test in spelling. Such an approach invites bias from regression to the mean effects and temporal changes (Torgerson and Torgerson 2008). Regression to the mean (RTM) is a group phenomenon. Children with low performance in a pre-test will tend, on average, to perform better on a subsequent test irrespective of any intervention effects, but simply due to the error component in the measurement of the first test. Temporal changes refer to improvement over time due to normal teaching or maturity. In addition to the potential problems from RTM and temporal changes in this research, both the pre- and post-tests were treatment inherent measures and therefore only able to measure specific improvement in skills directly taught, not general literacy skills such as reading comprehension.

Design

The randomised trial was undertaken with all pupils in Year seven during the school year 2004–5 in one school. We used a pragmatic approach: the setting was authentic and delivery of the intervention was in keeping with the pragmatic nature of the trial. So it was delivered by the pupils' usual teaching assistants, who had received training for this purpose from the designer of the programme. The children received the intervention *in addition to* their normal English lessons. Therefore this was an *add-on*, rather than a *replacement* intervention, and so 'business-as-usual' was appropriate as a control condition. It was important that the randomisation process was carried out independently of the assessment of the pupils, to avoid the possibility of selection bias due to the potential subversion of the randomisation process. All the guidelines in the CONSORT checklist were followed during design, conduct and reporting, such as including a trial-flow diagram in the report write-up, which showed the flow of all originally randomised participants through the process of the trial. The sample size was pre-determined by the number of children enrolled at the beginning of the school year. In the 2004 intake there were 155 new pupils, which was, therefore, the sample size. Nevertheless it was important to consider the likely effect size the sample would be able to detect and whether this was of 'educational significance'. On average educational interventions rarely produce effect sizes of half a standard deviation. The sample size in this study was large enough to give in excess of 80% power to observe as significant (2-tailed test with $p = 0.05$) an effect size of 0.5 (which requires a minimum sample size of 128 across the two groups). This sample size assumes no pre-test post-test correlation. In fact for most educational outcomes a correlation of at least 0.7 can be expected, which in practical terms implies an 'effective' sample size of about twice the number of participants actually randomised. Therefore, the study had greater than 90% power to show a difference of 0.5 of a standard deviation between the two groups.

Practicalities

The design of the trial was constrained by a number of practicalities. Firstly, timetabling constraints meant that the total amount of English time experienced by the experimental and control conditions was not equal. Each pupil in the intervention group received the programme for one hour per day for 10 consecutive school days in addition to their normal teaching; therefore whilst sometimes pupils received the programme during normal English classes, they also gave up time from other lessons to work through the programme. Overall, the children in the intervention group received slightly less normal classroom teaching in English, but substantially more teaching in literacy than usual because of the programme.

To avoid the possibility that control pupils might receive the intervention early all pupils received it via six laptops provided by the designer of the programme for this purpose. Access to the borrowed laptops was limited, and this enabled a practical justification for the random allocation to earlier or later exposure to the programme. As previously mentioned, the programme was delivered in the usual way by the teaching assistants, but their role was essentially to facilitate the children's use of the hardware and operating of the software, the instruction was entirely delivered through the programme in a uniform way.

Because access to the laptops and the programme was strictly controlled and supervised, potential leakage between the experimental and control groups was thought to be minimal. However, because the amount of time spent in standard English lessons during the intervention period was not measured and therefore not included in the analysis, we could not rule out this as a factor explaining the results.

Integrity

As previously mentioned, we used robust design, conduct and reporting for this trial, a large UK-based, individually randomised trial. For example, we used concealed allocation, and importantly stated this in the trial report. To achieve concealed allocation each child was given a unique code and the codes were sent to an independent researcher (from the York Trials Unit) who then randomly allocated them into the groups: intervention or control groups. Because the independent researcher did not have access to information about the characteristics of the children, selection bias could not occur by, for example, the researcher putting students with high test scores selectively into one of the groups. At all stages the tests were marked by persons 'blind' to individual pupils' group membership and independent of the school and the makers of the programme.

Similarly, the results were analysed by an independent statistician who was 'blind' to individual pupils' group membership. Consistency of marking was ensured by double marking of all of the scripts, with a check for inter-rater reliability. The primary and secondary outcome measures, spelling and reading, were pre-stated. The p value deemed significant for this comparison was 0.025 to allow for multiple testing (i.e. to reduce the possibility of a Type 1 error. Standardised age-appropriate measures (not previously used in the school) were used and the tests were not inherent to the intervention.

The trial demonstrated that, for the main outcome, spelling achievement, there was no difference between the two groups. For the secondary outcome, reading achievement, there was a statistically significant difference; however this favoured the control group.

The trial did have a number of important limitations. The main objective of assessing whether or not the software was good value and effective was addressed. However, because the trial had limited funding, potentially important secondary objectives, such as trying to disentangle the reasons *why* this particular software programme was less effective than standard practice were not illuminated. Additional funding for a complementary qualitative study may have been helpful, but funding constraints prevented this.

The trial was set within one school only. Whilst this school was a fairly typical state comprehensive school, generalisability to other schools in different geographical areas or to schools with different intake profiles etc. may be limited. Consequently it would have been better had it been possible to conduct the RCT across a number of schools, using a cluster design. In this scenario a large number of schools would have been randomised to receive or not receive the intervention. This design would have increased the ecological validity of the evaluation.

Conclusions

Trial based evaluations in educational research have been lacking in previous years, particularly in the UK. Recently there has been an upsurge in interest in trials by policy makers. In the US a large programme of trial-based research is underway funded by the Institute of Education Sciences (IES). The Institute of Education Sciences was established by The Education Sciences Reform Act of 2002 within the US Department of Education. Its mission is to provide rigorous evidence on which to base education practice and policy. In the UK the Department for Children, Schools and Families (DfCSF) has recently funded a large RCT-based national evaluation (led by the author and others at Durham University) of wave three of Every Child Counts, a one-to-one intensive numeracy intervention for 6- and 7-year-old children struggling with mathematics ('Numbers Count'). It is important, however, to capitalise on this renewed interest by ensuring that lessons painfully learnt from other areas where trials are more prevalent (e.g., health care research) are applied to this new era of trials in education. In particular a crucial aspect is transparent reporting of the trial methodology. Some journals now publish studies electronically, and at least for these the old issue of lack of journal space should no longer be a problem. Wholesale adoption of a slightly modified version of the CONSORT statement by trialists in education should be a priority. I have demonstrated that CONSORT criteria can be readily applied to an educational trial.

The ICT trial described was designed to fulfil the CONSORT criteria. These key methodological criteria developed for health care trials are readily applicable to educational trials as the essential principles are the same. As demonstrated here, it *is* possible to evaluate a widely-used intervention in a rigorous fashion and to obtain educationally meaningful results, which are of interest to the practitioner, policy maker and researcher.

In summary, rigorous trials are crucial to the development of evidence-based education. Poorly designed and reported trials are not helpful to anyone and can easily mislead. Applying the CONSORT statement to the design, conduct and reporting of a randomised controlled trial is an approach that can improve educational trials.

References

Altman, D.G. 1996. Better reporting of randomised controlled trials: The CONSORT statement. *British Medical Journal* 313: 570–1.

Boutron, I., D. Moher, D.G. Altman, K.F. Schulz, P. Ravaud, and for the CONSORT Group. 2008. Methods and processes of the CONSORT group: Example of an extension for trials assessing nonpharmacologic treatments. *Annals of Internal Medicine* 148: 295–309.

Brooks, G., J.N.V Miles, C.J. Torgerson, and D.J. Torgerson. 2006. Is an intervention using computer software effective in literacy learning? A randomised controlled trial. *Educational Studies* 32: 133–43.

Cook, T.D., and D. Campbell. 1979. *Quasi-experimentation: Design and analysis issues for field settings*. Boston: Houghton Miffling.

Fisher, R.A. 1971. *The design of experiments*. New York: Hafner Publishing Company.

Forsetlund, L., I. Chalmers, and A. Bjørndal. 2007. When was random allocation first used to generate comparison groups in experiments to assess the effects of social interventions? *Economics of Innovation and New Technology* 16, no. 5: 371–84.

Lindquist, E.F. 1940. *Statistical analysis in educational research*. Boston: Houghton Mifflin.

Moher, D., A. Jones, and L. Lepage. 2001. Use of the CONSORT statement and quality of reports of randomised trials. *Journal of the American Medical Association* 285: 1992–5.

Oakley, A. 2000. *Experiments in knowing: Eender and methodin the social sciences*. Cambridge: Polity Press.

Shadish, W.R., T.D. Cook, and T.D. Campbell. 2002. *Experimental and quasi-experimental designs for generalized causal inference*. Boston: Houghton-Mifflin Co.

Sheldon, T.A., and A. Oakley. 2002. Why we need randomised controlled trials. In *Clinical trials*, ed. L. Duley and B. Farrell, 13–24. London: BMJ Publishing.

Torgerson, C.J. 2003. *Systematic reviews*. London: Continuum.

Torgerson, C.J., and D. Elbourne. 2002. A systematic review and meta-analysis of the effectiveness of information and communication technology (ICT) on the teaching of spelling. *Journal of Research in Reading* 25: 129–43.

Torgerson, C.J., and D.J. Torgerson. 2001. The need for randomised controlled trials in educational research. *British Journal of Educational Studies* 49: 316–28.

Torgerson, D.J., and C.J. Torgerson. 2008. *The design of randomised trials in health, education and the social sciences*. Basingstoke: Palgrave, Macmillan.

Torgerson, C.J., and D. Zhu. 2003. A systematic review and meta-analysis of the effectiveness of ICT on literacy learning in English, 5–16. In *Research evidence in education library*. London: EPPI-Centre, Social Science Research Unit, Institute of Education, University of London.

Torgerson, C.J., and D. Zhu. 2004. A systematic review and meta-analysis of the effectiveness of ICT on literacy learning in English, 5–16. In *The impact of ICT on literacy education*, ed. R.J. Andrews. London: RoutledgeFalmer.

Walters, J.E. 1931. Seniors as counsellors. *The Journal of Higher Education* 2: 446–8.

Walters, J.E. 1932. Measuring effectiveness of personnel counseling. *Personnel Journal* 11: 227–36.

Evaluating the social impacts of inclusion through a multi-method research design

Elias Avramidis[a] and Alison Wilde[b]

[a]School of Education and Lifelong Learning, University of Exeter, UK; [b]Formerly at the University of York, UK

Although the development of policy towards inclusive education in the UK is well advanced, very little is known about the social outcomes of existing inclusive arrangements in primary settings. A recent study sought to fill this gap by systematically investigating the social impacts of inclusion on children accredited with Special Educational Needs (SEN) and their mainstream peers, while also identifying those educational practices contributing to increased social interaction and the development of friendships. Following a brief review of earlier research efforts and theoretical understandings that informed the design of our study, we present the mixed methodology employed which combined sociometric and psychometric techniques with more ecological qualitative methods. The ways in which these diverse methods complemented each other are discussed alongside wider methodological challenges germane to the research. We conclude by advocating the utilisation of interconnected methods, within a coherent research design of the sort described here.

Introduction

Inclusive education is now firmly established internationally as the main policy imperative with respect to children accredited with Special Educational Needs (SEN) or impairments (disabilities). In the UK, several policy initiatives (DfES 2001; DfES 2004) have vigorously supported the principle that children with SEN should, wherever possible, be educated in mainstream schools thus demonstrating the government's commitment to placing inclusive education at the heart of a wider agenda of social inclusion. Accordingly, recent legislation, such as the Special Educational Needs and Disability Act (2002), and the Equality Act and the Disability Equality Duty (2006), make discrimination against pupils on the basis of their disability unlawful, and thereby make real the right to education in mainstream schools for *all* pupils.

However, although the development of policy towards inclusion in the UK is well advanced, it is by no means all-encompassing. Specifically, the ambiguities contained in policy documents over whether 'inclusion' refers to *all* or *most* students have resulted in a variety of interpretations and applications across different Local

Authorities (LAs) and, most regrettably, the retention of separate special school provision. The continuing inability of mainstream schools to accommodate pupils with significant and complex needs has led many commentators in the field to be critical of a 'full' or 'purist' model of inclusion, and to embrace a more 'responsible' or 'moderate' form of it (Cigman 2007; Low 2007). Moreover, Baroness Mary Warnock (2005) expressed her reservations about inclusion on the basis of the high levels of bullying and victimisation reported by pupils with SEN compared to their typically developing peers. In so doing, Warnock argued that 'inclusion', viewed in terms of participation and belonging, can be accomplished in *any* setting. Interestingly, her assertion about bullying and generally poor social outcomes for pupils accredited with SEN was not backed up by sufficient empirical evidence, since the systematic assessment of the social and affective outcomes of inclusion in the UK has been lagging behind (Frederickson et al. 2007).

Indeed, most research efforts in the UK to date have been rooted within a school improvement tradition seeking to identify organisational structures and practices which may be associated with facilitating or impeding the development of inclusion. This work, however illuminating, has not evaluated systematically the social impacts of inclusive developments. Here we focus on the methodological approach adopted in a recent project which sought to fill this gap in the literature.

A brief review of existing research

Recent studies undertaken into special needs provision in the UK have often endeavoured to foreground disabled[1] students' voices in their emphasis upon the need for inclusion (Allan 1999; Watson and Davis 2002). Based upon wider disability studies approaches, these investigations have often taken a qualitative approach, favouring small-scale portraits of inclusion, or integration, 'in action'. Rather than 'just being there', inclusion is regarded as a process where systematic barriers to learning and participation are reduced, where each student is welcomed, valued and supported and where relationships are intentionally fostered (Booth and Ainscow 2002). Central to many such accounts is the idea that friendship is a crucial prerequisite for inclusion (Bunch and Valeo 2004) and concomitantly for 'cognitive growth and social development' (Forest and Lusthaus 1989, 45). Indeed, Koster et al. (2007) demonstrate that the social dimensions of schooling are central to parents' wishes for their children to attend mainstream, inclusion-orientated schools -echoing many disabled peoples' criticisms of segregated schooling and its adverse impacts upon wider social integration and inclusion (Sutherland 1991).

Whilst qualitative studies into the experiences of students with SEN have great value in articulating personal perceptions and accounts of school experience, they are limited in their capacity to capture the impacts of inclusion on the behaviour, social skills, attitude and friendships of children with and without SEN. With regard to behaviour and social skills, it has been reported that inclusion can bring about positive changes for all children (Cawley et al. 2002). Other studies examining attitudinal changes have found that mainstream pupils in inclusive classrooms show increased acceptance, understanding, and tolerance of individual differences (Capper and Pickett 1994; Fisher 1999; Shevlin and Moore 2000).

With regard to 'social status' and 'friendships', it is consistently reported that integrated disabled children have lower status, are less accepted and more rejected by their classmates (Larrivee and Horne 1991; Vaughn, Elbaum, and Schumm 1996).

For example, an American review of 17 studies which used sociometric ratings to compare pupils accredited with SEN to their mainstream peers (Ochoa and Olvarez 1995) concluded that the former had significantly reduced social status. Similarly, in another US study, Pavri and Luftig (2000) found that 11-year-old pupils with learning difficulties were less popular, experienced more loneliness and were less socially accepted than those without learning impairments. Similar findings have been found across different national school systems including the UK (Frederickson and Furnham 1998), Holland (Scheepstra, Nakken, and Pijl 1999), Norway (Frostad and Pijl 2007), Spain (Cambra and Silvestre 2003) and Israel (Tur-Kaspa, Margalit, and Most 1999). Furthermore, it is commonly reported that pupils with motor impairments and pupils with intellectual impairments have fewer problems in their contact with peers than pupils with behaviour problems or pupils with autism (Mand 2007; De Monchy, Pijl, and Zandberg 2004; Champerlain, Kasari, and Rotheram-Fuller 2007). Other studies, however, have shown that, despite their generally low social status, children accredited with learning difficulties had managed to form and maintain some positive social relationships in inclusive settings and felt part of a social network (Pavri and Monda-Amaya 2001; Meyer 2001).

Given the dearth of similar studies in the UK context, it was timely that a large-scale study evaluating the social impacts of inclusion on pupils accredited with SEN and their mainstream peers be conducted. The two main theoretical understandings that informed the design of our study were the '*homophily*' and '*contact*' hypotheses. The *homophily* hypothesis (McPherson, Smith-Lovin, and Cook 2001) concerns the commonly reported tendency in research on students' social relations, for students to prefer to associate with 'similar' peers. Homophily is likely to be based on different dimensions of identity, such as age, gender, race, educational attainment, values, interests, and beliefs. It has been argued that because pupils attributed with significant SEN often lack certain qualities on one or more of the dimensions for homophily, they tend to be excluded by pupils without SEN who in turn flock together (Guralnick et al. 1995).

The 'homophily' hypothesis is also referred to in the literature as the '*similarity hypothesis*' (Male 2007). Male distinguishes between three types of similarity: *attitude similarity, demographic similarity* (for example, age, gender, socioeconomic status) and *similarity in personality*. Drawing on child development and personality literature, she outlines why similarity is an important condition for friendship formation:

- if we like those who are similar to us, there is a good chance that they will like us;
- communication is easier with people who are similar;
- similar others may confirm the rightness of our attitudes and beliefs; and
- it makes sense if we like ourselves, then we should also like others who are similar to us. (Male 2007, 463–64)

The *homophily* or *similarity* hypothesis largely explains why even in inclusive settings children with learning difficulties and/or disabilities are more likely to form friendships amongst themselves, on the basis of their shared experiences of disabling barriers rather than with their typically developing peers. This is particularly true in situations where children with special needs spend considerable time in withdrawal settings such as units embedded in mainstream schools ('resource rooms' in US terminology).

By contrast, the *contact* hypothesis refers to the effect of increased interaction on the mainstream pupils' attitudes towards pupils they perceive as having SEN. According to the '*contact hypothesis*' (Yuker 1988), as mainstream pupils in schools implementing inclusion programmes get closer to their (formally) marginalised peers, their attitudes become more positive. Indeed, several researchers have suggested that the attitude of typically developing peers can be influenced (Capper and Pickett 1994; Scheepstra, Nakken, and Pijl 1999) thus giving empirical support to the contact hypothesis. Moreover, research has also shown that co-operative learning arrangements foster co-operation between children with and without SEN and have considerable strength in promoting attitudinal changes in both groups of pupils (Gartin, Murdick, and Digby 1992). However, as Pijl, Frostad, and Flemm (2008) remind us, including pupils with special needs does not automatically lead to an increase of friendships between themselves and their typical counterparts:

> ...physical integration is only a very basic condition (and) ... becoming part of the group is not an automatism and ... pupils with special needs in particular may need extra support in group participation. Support could focus on the peers, the teachers, the pupils with special needs or the school organisation. What support is most effective in what situation is as yet a largely open question (Pijl, Frostad, and Flemm 2008, 403).

Indeed, it is likely that divisions will be perpetuated and perceptions of difference confirmed, where school cultures maintain stereotypical knowledge of disabled people and their impairments. Further, it is worth noting here that the social psychological literature contains numerous experimental studies where simply increasing contact did not produce any attitudinal change or even resulted in undesirable consequences.[2] In this respect, the contact hypothesis should be viewed with caution.

Clearly, friendships cannot be engineered but helping children find creative ways to form them should be at the top of every school's agenda. Consequently, in testing the *homophily* and *contact* hypotheses in primary settings at different stages of inclusive development, our emphasis was placed on how disabling environments contribute to the social marginalisation and isolation of children designated with SEN; and, crucially, on identifying the institutional practices that facilitate the formation of positive social relationships. In this respect, our study had an applied dimension by way of providing promising pointers to developing inclusive school cultures.

Aims and research questions of the study

The principal aim of the study was to investigate the social position of pupils accredited with SEN in mainstream settings and their perceived self-concept. The study sought to address the following research questions:

- What are the predominant patterns of friendship and social interaction found in mainstream primary schools at different stages of inclusive development?
- What types of social position do children with special needs occupy within these social networks? And what perceptions do they hold about their self-concept?
- How do the identified patterns of affiliation vary according to severity of need, gender, and social demographics? And to what extent can these be attributed to the school's culture, ethos, approach to inclusion, and teachers' practices?

Research design

Fieldwork was conducted in seven primary schools in one Local Education Authority (LEA) in the North of England. Our selection of a suitable sample of schools was informed by the number of children accredited with SEN and the range of impairments present in the schools' registers. Further, our sample consisted of schools which took different 'tracks' towards inclusion with a view to assessing the effectiveness of their formal approaches. Hence, in choosing seven schools, we took care to include two schools with resource units of different types, and one school which took an active part in supporting dual placements, which were designed to culminate in full mainstream integration. Two of the remaining four schools were chosen on the basis of an examination of their Office for Standards in Education (Ofsted) reports, evaluated with indices for inclusion taken from the Index for Inclusion (Booth and Ainscow 2002). These schools were drawn from a long list of potential schools discussed with the LA and determined by the numbers of children accredited with special needs, with statements, or on School Action, or School Action Plus. As there was a bias in this larger sample towards schools in suburban areas, a further school was chosen from a less economically advantaged area. Finally, a seventh school was chosen (also drawn from the long list) because it had given us a very positive expression of desire to be included in the study, following the receipt of our invitation to all schools in the area. All pupils enrolled in years 5 and 6 participated in the study resulting in a total sample of 566 children. It is worth noting here that the selected schools were drawn from a predominantly white middle-class LA, and therefore, could be regarded as fairly homogeneous 'clusters' in the sense of catering for children of the same ethnic and socio-economic background. Had the study been conducted in a multicultural area, the ethnic dimension would have been a significant factor affecting the children's process of socialisation.

The study adopted a multi-method research design consisting of sociometric techniques ascertaining the social position of pupils accredited with SEN and detecting the predominant patterns of friendship and social interaction in their classrooms; a psychometric assessment of pupils' perceptions of themselves resulting in an in-depth exploration of the multidimensional nature of their self-concepts; and qualitative interviewing of professionals in the seven participating schools with a view to examining individual (teacher) and institutional approaches to inclusion. It is towards discussing the application of these diverse approaches in our study that we turn next.

Utilising a psychometric approach

Psychometric approaches have played a key role in evaluating the affective and social outcomes of inclusion especially in the US. This quantitatively-orientated literature has traditionally sought to ascertain pupils' attitudes towards other pupils and themselves. Reflecting different cultural concerns and disciplinary origins, most significantly *individualistic* rather than *social* models of disability, there is a greater focus on larger scale studies of student perceptions, which often privilege psychological orientations. This perspective is often closely related to explanations of educational need which are anchored in an individualist or even 'deficit' model of student sociality. However, relating a number of self-concept domains to educational environments, many of these studies evaluate self-perceptions taking account of social contexts.

Psychometric instruments are often used in educational research to measure a number of areas of personality, in particular, facets of self-concept. These investigations take a number of forms, including estimations of academic, social, and general worth. In particular, although there is considerable consensus that pupils with learning difficulties have comparatively negative *academic* self-concepts, there is significant disagreement throughout a range of conflicting studies into the *social* and *general* self-concept of children accredited with learning difficulties or special needs (see Zeleke 2004, for a comprehensive review). Considering the heterogeneous range of learning difficulties, special needs and educational arrangements included within these studies, it is unsurprising that a wide variety of findings have been reported. Moreover, Bear, Minke, and Manning (2002) demonstrated in their meta-analysis of the relevant literature, how the instruments used had a significant effect on the production of conflicting or contradictory results. In particular, they demonstrated that the Piers-Harris Children's Self-Concept Scale (Piers 1969) was used in many studies before 1986, providing uni-dimensional findings and was theoretically and empirically inadequate (Bear, Minke, and Manning 2002, 406). By contrast, more recent multidimensional instruments, far from assuming a single form of self-concept, apply ratings across a range of domains. In addition to academic, social and general worth, it is acknowledged that confidence in other areas (such as athletic skills, physical appearance, and talents) and support from other people may elevate otherwise lower self-perceptions.

In choosing, therefore, the psychometric instrument most suited to examining self-concepts within a social context, it was deemed essential that the items on the scale emphasise the multi-dimensionality of the construct, particularly since we sought to extrapolate more relational understandings of self-concept. Of the multi-dimensional instruments identified the Self-Perception Profile for Children (SPPC)[3] developed by Susan Harter (Harter 1985) had the least limitations and corresponded most closely to the aims of our study, especially in individualistic, 'what's inside their heads' terms' (Goodley 2007).

Utilising a sociometric approach

Sociometric instruments are quantitative tools which are designed to measure social relationships, typically used in education studies to understand group clusters and characteristics and for evaluating the extent and types of students' popularity within classrooms. The peer nomination approach originated by Moreno (1934) has been the most commonly used sociometric technique. It requires children to name classmates who fit a particular sociometric criterion (e.g. 'Name three classmates with whom you like to play'). Nominations may be based on positive criteria (as in the example above) as well as negative criteria (e.g. 'Name three classmates with whom you do not like to play') and they have generally been found to be stable over time among primary school children (Asher and Taylor 1981; Vaughn, Elbaum, and Schumm 1996). Popularity is usually measured on a continuum and it is positioned between two poles: popular and rejected. Common additions to this are average, controversial, and neglected statuses. These latter categories are often linked to typical behaviour attributed to those labelled with emotional and behavioural difficulties, thus there is an association of externalising behaviours, which are considered to be disruptive, with the statuses of controversial or rejected. Even though sociometric methods often confirm or extend these associations, ascertaining the causal relationship between status and behaviour is difficult; and, dependent on the instrument used, relationships between general popularity, and membership of clusters is often unclear (Farmer and Farmer 1996).

A further limitation of the peer nomination method is that children deemed to have SEN or impairments are likely to be overlooked (Larrivee and Horne 1991). As such, this method often results in findings which highlight the popularity or marginalisation of a limited number of children; this is most likely to reflect the normative standards of the class whilst obscuring the position of children accredited with SEN. To avoid such bias inherent within the peer nomination method, researchers have instead utilised the 'rating scale' sociometric method, which asks each pupil to rate *all* their classmates on a Likert scale (i.e. degree of preference for spending time with a person). Rating scale studies place equal attention on each class member, therefore providing a 'whole class', multi-dimensional picture of group associations and the reasons behind them. Such studies have the capacity to illustrate the formation of social clusters within classrooms, thus offering a more coherent picture of how pupils designated with SEN are viewed and treated by their classmates (see, for example, Stanovich, Jordan, and Perot 1998). However, they also carry a significant weakness since they often ask children to identify those whom they do not like or whom they would prefer 'to be more like other people', thus reinforcing popular prejudices within the school culture and further demarcating some children as different.

Finally, a more nuanced sociometric approach is the one utilised by Farmer and Farmer (1996). Although their particular approach involved the nomination of three peers and the inclusion of potentially negative questions, the questions asked were much more conducive to providing data on the character of relationships. That is, eight descriptors were given to students, excavating important aspects underlying social preference and the conditions and processes shaping social influence. Two of the eight descriptors (i.e. 'starting fights' and 'disruptive') had negatively biased connotations. The other descriptors were: 'co-operative', 'popular', 'athletic', 'leaders', 'good at schoolwork' and 'shy/withdrawn'.[4] This nominating technique was carried out by Farmer and Farmer alongside a social network assessment question (*'Are there some kids here in your classroom who hang around together a lot?'*). In synthesising the descriptors with this question they were able to provide a clear picture of homophilous clusters, demonstrating the social compositions and bases for affiliation.

In selecting the sociometric instruments, a central consideration was their capacity to ask questions which locate the students in disabling environments, rather than positioning children as the 'problem' or the causal factor of them. In this, we decided to avoid 'peer rejection' explanations due to their pathological implications, in favour of understanding the social and cultural conditions underlying the constitution of social networks. Far from simply obtaining numerical data indicating hierarchies of popularity, we were concerned with understanding the processes and conditions which contribute to the shaping of social networks. To understand the characteristics which lead people to make some preferences for peer affiliation rather than others, we combined a classic peer nomination technique (*Who are your five best friends in your classroom?*) with Farmer and Farmer's (1996) approach, which involves peer nomination on the basis of eight descriptors followed by an additional social network assessment question. To avoid potential ethical problems inherent in sociometric research, the process of 'nomination' formed a small part of a much broader interview addressing a wide range of issues, thus minimising the chance of pupils sharing their nominations. Similarly, particular attention was paid to the psychometric part of the study, where the administration of the self-report instrument was made during structured lessons and in an inclusive manner.

Collecting qualitative evidence

Our synthesis of sociometric and psychometric techniques achieved our objective of finding a more balanced quantitative approach which could shed more light on both the social and affective outcomes of inclusion. However, it was imperative from the outset to ensure that our sociometric and psychometric methods were embedded in a wider 'naturalistic' research design. For this reason, we began our study with an examination of the selected schools' Ofsted reports and inclusion policies, followed by interviewing 27 Key Stage 2 teachers, including the school Special Educational Needs Coordinators (SENCOs). These interviews were guided by a semi-structured schedule, which consisted of questions eliciting the respondents' understanding of inclusion; their knowledge of and attitudes towards national and local inclusion initiatives; their perceptions of barriers and factors affecting the successful implementation of inclusion; their perceived academic and social outcomes of the process; and, finally, their most innovative practices for enhancing social interaction between pupils and facilitating the formation of heterogeneous clusters of affiliation. This evidence was supplemented with participant observations conducted in various school contexts (e.g. in the class, in the playground etc). The decision to employ these ecological methods at the outset, reflected our desire to counteract the reductionism inherent in solely quantitative research designs, by gaining rich insights into our participating schools' culture and practices (Bourdieu and Wacquant 1992).

In addition to the fieldwork described above, rich qualitative data were obtained through our interviews with pupils. As already mentioned, our sociometric assessment formed a small part of a much broader one-to-one interview addressing a wide range of issues including attitudes to schooling; teaching and learning processes; positive and negative experiences; perceptions of friendship networks; and associated aspects of classroom culture. This evidence, coupled with other personal information (i.e. length of time registered in the school, family circumstances) was invaluable in interpreting the quantitative findings.

Combining the evidence gathered from diverse approaches

It is clearly not possible to present in detail the outcomes of this study in the space of this article. However, at the risk of being reductive, it is possible to briefly present some outcomes with a view to demonstrating the ways in which the diverse methods employed complemented each other.

Pupils designated with SEN were found to have lower perceptions of self-concept, to be less popular, and to have fewer friends than their typically developing peers. However, statistically significant differences between the two groups were only detected in three out of seven schools. To interpret these differences between settings we delved into our qualitative database and examined the 'individual' and 'institutional' approaches to inclusion. In so doing, we identified a continuum of approaches across the seven schools, ranging from inclusive to integrationist and to exclusionary stances. In this way, the quantitative findings were interpreted through the identified 'enabling' or 'restricted' practices and circumstances in the participating schools.

Another important finding concerned the degree of our pupils' participation in the social life of their classroom network and the identification of 'isolated' cases in our sample. Following Pijl, Frostad, and Flemm (2008), our participants' participation in their classrooms was assessed through three indexes for social inclusion: peer acceptance, friendships and membership of a cohesive subgroup. Pupils were categorised as socially included if they were accepted by their peers, had at least one mutual relationship, and belonged to a coherent subgroup. The analysis revealed similar percentages of 'excluded' SEN and non-SEN pupils, indicating that despite their generally low social status, pupils with SEN had managed to form some positive relationships and were part of a social network. Here, the qualitative evidence gathered through the student interviews was instrumental in elaborating the conditions contributing to the social isolation of individual pupils (both those designated with SEN and those without).

Finally, the research did not provide support to the theory of 'homophily' with regard to SEN status; that is, the commonly made assumption in the inclusion literature that pupils with SEN would cluster together was not supported by our sociometric data. In this respect, SEN was not found to be a significant dimension of difference determining the composition of subgroups. It is worth clarifying here that Social Network Analysis (SNA) as a quantitative method is *not* predicated on hypothesis testing; rather the analysis is 'relational' in the sense of identifying patterns of social groupings between individuals ('clusters') in a given classroom. These results are not explicable within the dataset (classroom network) and additional qualitative evidence about the context and the processes of affiliation and group formation at play is needed to interpret them. The analysis of the qualitative evidence collected through the student interviews enhanced, therefore, the explanatory adequacy of the research design, since our quantitative investigation of patterns of social grouping was related to the empirical world of the school in its natural, ongoing character.

Concluding remark: moving beyond the sterile quantitative vs. qualitative debate

The quantitative-qualitative divide in educational, sociological and psychological research is alive and well (Denzin and Lincoln 2005). The two paradigms (positivism/postpositivism and interpretivism/constructivism) are distinguished by opposing ontologies and epistemologies, which differ at the level of analysis, not at the level of methodologies or methods, in that numerical/statistical or textual data collection methods can be interpreted within both paradigms. Philosophically, the two paradigms are irreconcilable and instead of engaging in a dialogue of the deaf, we need to explore innovative methodological approaches which involve the application of mixed methods within the same project in a complementary manner. Here, a particularly useful concept originally coined by Levi-Strauss (1966) to describe a multi-method research approach such as the one adopted in our study of the social impacts of inclusion, is the researcher as a *bricoleur*.

A bricoleur is a *'Jack of all trades or a kind of professional do it yourself person'* (Levi-Strauss 1966, 17). That is, a *bricoleur* will deploy a wide range of interconnected methods, hoping always to get a better fix on the subject matter at hand. The outcome of the *bricoleur's* method is the *bricolage*; a pieced-together, close-knit set of practices that provide solutions to a problem in a concrete situation.

It is worth noting here that the *bricolage*, according to Levi-Strauss, is an emergent construction that changes and takes new forms, as different tools, methods, and techniques are added to the puzzle. In this respect, it requires the researcher to remain reflective throughout the research process and not become tied to a predetermined, stable and unchanging research design. However, although the *bricoleur's* choice of tools and research practices is not strictly set in advance, it should not be taken as a form of 'naïve eclecticism'; rather, the *bricolage* is a set of interconnected methods aimed at addressing specific research objectives, and as such it represents a coherent research design.

Our examination of the social impacts of inclusion policies and approaches on pupils' experiences has, therefore, synthesised psychometric and sociometric instruments with more inductive, open-ended enquiries to gain a more multi-dimensional view of inclusion. These strategic research choices have allowed us to conduct an investigation, which is able to identify processes that highlight the interplay of personal and social selves in a social context. It is our contention that the field of educational research would benefit from the increased utilisation of coherent multi-method research designs of the type described here.

Acknowledgement

The research on which this article was based (*The social impacts of inclusion on pupils with SEN and their mainstream peers*, 2006–2009 – Award Reference: RES-061-23-0069-A) was funded by the Economic and Social Research Council, whose support is gratefully acknowledged.

Notes

1. We are using the term disabled here and elsewhere according to a 'social model of disability'. As such, this term includes children with accredited impairments and those that are otherwise identified as having Special Educational Needs.
2. For example, in Sherif's famous summer camp experiment, the competition for resources between the two participating groups of children resulted in conflict, negative prejudices and aggressive behaviour. It was only when the two groups were forced to work together to reach common goals that prejudice and tension amongst them eased (Sherif et al. 1988).
3. The SPPC contains six separate subscales tapping five specific domains (Scholastic Competence, Social Acceptance, Athletic Competence, Physical Appearance, and Behavioural Conduct) as well as global self-worth.
4. This category could, of course, have negative or positive connotations but is less pejorative than the 'disruptive' and 'starts fights' categories.

References

Allan, J. 1999. *Actively seeking inclusion*. London: Falmer.

Asher, S.R., and A.R. Taylor. 1981. Social outcomes of mainstreaming: Sociometric assessment and beyond. *Exceptional Education Quarterly* 1, no. 4: 13–30.

Bear, G., K.M. Minke, and M.A. Manning. 2002. Self-Concept of students with learning disabilities: A meta-analysis. *School Psychology Review* 31, no. 3: 405–27.

Booth, T., and M. Ainscow. 2002. *Index for Inclusion: Developing learning and inclusion in schools*. Bristol: Centre for Studies on Inclusive Education.

Bourdieu, P., and J.D. Wacquant. 1992. *An invitation to reflexive sociology*. Chicago: University of Chicago Press.

Bunch, G., and A. Valeo. 2004. Student attitudes towards peers with disabilities in inclusive and special education schools. *Disability and Society* 19, no. 1: 61–76.

Cambra, C., and N. Silvestre. 2003. Students with SEN in the inclusive classroom: Social integration and self-concept. *European Journal of Special Needs Education* 18, no. 2: 197–208.

Capper, C.A., and R.S. Pickett. 1994. The relationship between school structure and culture and students' views of diversity and inclusive education. *The Special Education Leadership Review* 2: 102–22.

Cawley, J., S. Hayden, E. Cade, and S. Baker-Kroczynski. 2002. Including students with disabilities into the general education science classroom. *Exceptional Children* 60, no. 4: 423–33.

Champerlain, B., C. Kasari, and E. Rotheram-Fuller. 2007. Involvement or isolation: The social networks of children with autism in regular classrooms. *Journal of Autism and Developmental Disorders* 37, no. 2: 230–42.

Cigman, R. 2007. Editorial introduction. In *Included or excluded? The challenge of the mainstream for some SEN children*, ed. R. Cigman. London: Routledge.

De Monchy, M., S.J. Pijl, and T. Zandberg. 2004. Discrepancies in judging social inclusion and bullying of pupils with behaviour problems. *European Journal of Special Needs Education* 19, no. 3: 317–13.

Denzin, N., and Y. Lincoln. 2005. *The Sage handbook of qualitative research*. Thousand Oaks, CA: Sage.

Department for Education and Skills (DfES). 2001. *Inclusive schooling: Children with Special Educational Needs*. London: DfES.

Department for Education and Skills (DfES). 2004. *Removing barriers to achievement. The government's strategy on SEN*. London: DfES.

Disability Equality Duty. 2006. http://www.dotheduty.org/ (accessed September 1, 2008).

Equality Act. 2006. http://www.opsi.gov.uk/acts/acts2006/pdf/ukpga_20060003_en.pdf (accessed September 1, 2008).

Farmer, T.W., and E.M.Z. Farmer. 1996. Social relationships of students with exceptionalities in mainstream classrooms: Social networks and homophily. *Exceptional Children* 62, no. 5: 431–50.

Fisher, D. 1999. According to their peers: Inclusion as high school students see it. *Mental Retardation* 37, no. 6: 458–67.

Forest, M., and E. Lusthaus. 1989. Promoting educational equality for all students. In *Educating all students in the mainstream of regular education*, ed. S. Stainback, W. Stainback, and M. Forest. Baltimore, MD: Paul H Brookes.

Frederickson, N., and A. Furnham. 1998. Sociometric classification methods in school peer groups: a comparative investigation. *Journal of Child Psychology and Psychiatry* 39, no. 6: 921–34.

Frederickson, N., E. Simmonds, L. Evans, and C. Soulsby. 2007. Assessing the social and affective outcomes of inclusion. *British Journal of Special Education* 34, no. 2: 105–15.

Frostad, P., and S.J. Pijl. 2007. Does being friendly help in making friends? The relation between the social position and social skills of pupils with special needs in mainstream education. *European Journal of Special Needs Education* 22, no. 1: 15–30.

Gartin, B.C., N.L. Murdick, and A.D. Digby. 1992. Cooperative activities to assist in the integration of students with disabilities. *Journal of Instructional Psychology* 19, no. 4: 241–45.

Goodley, D. 2007. Towards socially just pedagogies: Deleuzoguattarian critical disability studies. *International Journal of Inclusive Education* 11, no. 3: 317–34.

Guralnick, M.J., R.T. Connor, M. Hammond, J.M. Gottman, and K. Kinnish. 1995. Immediate effects of mainstreamed settings on social interactions and social integration of preschool children. *American Journal on Mental Retardation* 100, no. 4: 359–77.

Harter, S. 1985. *Manual for the self-perception profile for children*. Denver: University of Denver.

Koster, M., S.J Pijl, H. van Houten, and H. Nakken. 2007. The social position and development of pupils with SEN in mainstream Dutch primary schools. *European Journal of Special Needs Education* 22, no. 1: 31–46.

Larrivee, B., and M.D. Horne. 1991. Social status: A comparison of mainstreamed students with peers of different ability levels. *The Journal of Special Education* 25, no. 1: 90–101.

Levi-Strauss, C. 1966. *The savage mind*. Chicago: University of Chicago Press.

Low, C. 2007. A defence of moderate inclusion and the end of ideology. In *Included or excluded? The challenge of the mainstream for some SEN children*, ed. R. Cigman. London: Routledge.

Male, D. 2007. The friendships and peer relationships of children and young people who experience difficulties in learning. In *The sage handbook of special education*, ed. L. Florian. London: Sage.

Mand, J. 2007. Social position of special needs pupils in the classroom: A comparison between German special schools for pupils with learning difficulties and integrated primary school classes. *European Journal of Special Needs Education* 22, no. 1: 6–14.

McPherson, M., L. Smith-Lovin, and J.M. Cook. 2001. Birds of a feather: Homophily in social networks. *Annual Review of Sociology* 27: 415–44.

Meyer, L.H. 2001. The impact of inclusion on children's lives: Multiple outcomes and friendships in particular. *International Journal of Disability, Development and Education* 48, no. 1: 2009–31.

Moreno, J.L. 1934. *Who shall survive: A new approach to the problem of human interrelations*. Washington, DC: Nervous and Mental Disease publishing.

Ochoa, S.H., and A. Olvarez. 1995. Meta-analysis of peer rating sociometric studies of pupils with LD. *Journal of Special Education* 29, no. 1: 1–19.

Pavri, S., and R. Luftig. 2000. The social face of inclusive education: Are students with LD really included in the classroom? *Preventing School Failure* 45, no. 1: 8–14.

Pavri, S., and L. Monda-Amaya. 2001. Social support in inclusive schools: Students' and teachers' perspectives. *Exceptional Children* 67, no. 3: 391–411.

Piers, E.V. 1969. *Manual for the Piers-Harris children's self concept scale*. Nashville, TN: Counselor Recordings and Tests.

Pijl, S.J., P. Frostad, and A. Flemm. 2008. The Social Position of Pupils with Special Needs in Regular Schools. *Scandinavian Journal of Educational Research* 52, no. 4: 387–405.

Scheepstra, A.J.M., H. Nakken, and S.J. Pijl. 1999. Contract with classmates: The social position of pupils with Down's syndrome in Dutch mainstream education. *European Journal of Special Needs Education* 14, no. 3: 212–20.

Sherif, M., O.J. Harvey, B.J. White, W. Hood, and C. Sherif. 1988. *The Robber's Cave Experiment: Intergroup conflict and cooperation*. Connecticut: Wesleyan University Press.

Shevlin, M., and M. Moore. 2000. Creating opportunities for contact between mainstream pupils and their counterparts with learning difficulties. *British Journal of Special Education* 27, no. 1: 29–34.

Special Educational Needs and Disability Act. 2002. http://www.opsi.gov.uk/ACTS/acts2001/ukpga_20010010_en_1 (accessed September 1, 2008).

Stanovich, P.J., A. Jordan, and J. Perot. 1998. Relative differences in academic self- concept and peer acceptance among students in inclusive classrooms. *Remedial and Special Education* 19, no. 2: 120–26.

Sutherland, A. 1991. *Disabled we stand*. Brookline books.

Tur-Kaspa, H., M. Margalit, and T. Most. 1999. Reciprocal friendship, reciprocal rejection and socio-emotional adjustment: The social experiences of children with learning disorders over a one-year period. *European Journal of Special Needs Education* 14, no. 1: 17–48.

Vaughn, S., B.E. Elbaum, and J.S. Schumm. 1996. The effects of inclusion on the social functioning of students with learning disabilities. *Journal of Learning Disabilities* 29, no. 6: 598–608.

Warnock, M. 2005. *Special Educational Needs: A new look*. London: Philosophy of Education Society of Great Britain.

Watson, N., and J. Davis. 2002. *Countering stereotypes of disability: Disabled children and resistance*. London: Continuum.

Yuker, H.E. 1988. The effects of contact on attitudes toward disabled persons: Some empirical generalisations. In *Attitudes toward persons with disabilities*, ed. H.E. Yuker, 262–74. New York: Springer.

Zeleke, S. 2004. Self-concepts of students with learning disabilities and their normally achieving peers: A review. *European Journal of Special Needs Education* 19, no. 2: 145–70.

Researching 'teachers in the news': the portrayal of teachers in the British national and regional press

Anders Hansen

Department of Media and Communication, University of Leicester, UK

An outline of frameworks for conceptualising and analysing news media roles in the representation of teachers, is followed by a discussion of quantitative and qualitative approaches to the study of news coverage. An argument is made for the benefit of using corpus linguistic tools within the overall conceptual focus on lexical and syntactical structures offered by critical discourse analysis. Findings are presented from a comprehensive study of the press portrayal of teachers and education. Focusing on the portrayal of teachers in news headline coverage, the study shows a considerable lexical and syntactic change between 1991 and 2005 in the public/news representation of teachers, broadly from a negative view of teachers as troublesome to a more positive emphasis on teachers as a hard-working profession besieged by mounting pressures.

Introduction

The media, both national and local, are an important public arena for the articulation and contestation of education issues and professional identities. Concern about the media's role in shaping and influencing public images of teachers and education is neither particularly recent (e.g. Ball 1990; Wallace 1993), nor is it a particularly British phenomenon (e.g. Blackmore 2004; Maeroff 1998). But while numerous studies have examined the portrayal of teachers in film and other entertainment media content (e.g. Dalton 2003; Ellismore 2005), including the mapping of changes in such images over time, there have been surprisingly few longitudinal studies of that most prominent and politically important genre of media content: news.

Important exceptions to this dearth of longitudinal research are Matilda Wiklund's research on how representations of teachers in a leading Swedish newspaper have changed since the early 1980s (Wiklund 2003), and Peter Cunningham's (1992) study of changing British press presentations of teachers and education over the years 1950, 1970 and 1990. Such mapping of changing media images provides an important component for examining the relationship between changes in media images and changes in public perceptions, as established for example through regularly conducted opinion surveys.

The media, public opinion, policy-making and professional groups' perceptions all interact in complex ways, far removed from any simple cause-effect relationships. While there has been little research specifically on media roles in relation to public images of teachers, there is considerable evidence from comparable fields (including studies of media representation of social workers, e.g. Franklin 1998, 1999) that the news media are important in terms of creating 'climates of opinion', public agendas, and in terms of drawing the boundaries for public debate and discussion.

Studies comparing public opinion poll data with media reporting provide some indication of the key factors (e.g. the degree of diversity of definitions across different media, the extent to which the public can draw on direct experience or alternative sources of information, etc.) which determine the extent of media influence on public opinion (Lacey and Longman 1997; Zaller 1992). A focus on media influence on public understanding and opinion, however, also raises questions about the range of voices and definitions in media reporting, including questions about the practices and factors which influence whose definitions get onto the media agenda, and how those definitions then fare in the public arena (McCombs 2004; Hilgartner and Bosk 1988).

Of particular relevance in this context is Wiklund's demonstration of the 'voices' who most prominently contribute to public and press images of teachers, namely politicians and interest groups, followed, less prominently and with greater variation over the period, by teachers, experts and lay citizens. Equally of interest is the finding that by the early 2000s, the themes and issues associated with news coverage of teachers, in the Swedish press, revolve around the key notion of a well qualified and proud profession '... forced to act as administrator, police, social worker and psychologist, instead of functioning as the transmitter of knowledge [it] ought to be' and threatened '... by the educational politics from the government, by the municipal politicians, by violence, poor working conditions and low salary ...' (Wiklund 2003, 14).

Relevant frameworks for analysing the media roles in relation to public definitions and public understanding of teachers and education issues thus include media and public opinion research, agenda-building/agenda-setting research as well as work on the construction of social problems and the construction of news. Core to several of these frameworks is the concept of framing as it has been developed and elaborated in communications research over recent decades (Gamson 1985; Entman 1993; Reese 2001). As Entman (1993) has argued, framing in media discourse works principally at two levels: *selection* and *salience*. The media draw attention to particular issues, actors, definitions and interpretations through (1) *selection* (e.g. our attention is drawn to some aspects while others, not selected, are kept out of public view), and (2) through the way in which these are *presented*, with particular *emphases, syntactical* and *lexical* choices, which in turn promote particular definitions and interpretations rather than others.

Aims, methods and sample

The research reported here is drawn from a comprehensive news-study, which formed part of a larger study of the Status of Teachers (Hargreaves et al. 2007).

The general objective of the news-study was to provide a comprehensive mapping of teacher/education portrayal in the news, to complement the evidence from the larger study's surveys of public and professional perceptions of the status of teachers. The news-study combined quantitative and qualitative approaches to the analysis of media coverage:

(1) A systematic quantitative *content analysis*, focusing specifically on *themes* and *actors/voices* in national and regional press coverage of teachers and education.
(2) A longitudinal analysis, drawing from both corpus linguistics (e.g. Stubbs 1996) and from critical discourse analysis (e.g. Fowler 1991; Fairclough 2003), of the representation of teachers in newspaper headlines in the period 1991 through 2005.

This contribution focuses on the second of these two analyses. A key objective of the analysis presented here was to retain the rigorous and systematic features of content analysis, while at the same time allowing for a much more detailed and sensitive exploration (than is possible within content analysis) of how the 'meaning' of teachers is (ideologically) constructed through particular lexical and syntactic choices, i.e. the core foci of critical linguistic analysis (e.g. Fowler 1991; Hodge and Kress 1993).

Where the strength of content analysis resides in its ability to deal with large bodies of text in a systematic and reliable fashion, the often much more insightful observations made in critical discourse analysis have traditionally been impeded by its narrow focus on a small number of selected texts and the concomitant twin problems of: (1) establishing how representative such texts are of a wider discourse *and* (2) missing the kind of repetitive lexical or syntactic patterns that only become visible when looking at large bodies of text. The latter is precisely one of the key arguments for a corpus linguistic approach to critical discourse analysis, 'allowing researchers to objectively identify widespread patterns of naturally occurring language and rare but telling examples, both of which may be over-looked by a small-scale analysis. Such language patterns can help to illuminate the existence of discourses that may otherwise be unobserved' (Baker and McEnery 2005). 'Corpus linguistics' thus, for the purposes of this analysis, is defined as the systematic computer-assisted analysis of selected linguistic patterns in a naturally occurring and carefully selected corpus of text, in this case newspaper text (see also Biber, Conrad, and Reppen 1998, 4).

The present analysis seeks particularly to explore how teachers are represented in newspapers by examining the lexical and syntactic patterns associated with the two keywords 'teacher' and 'teachers'. The lexical analysis focuses on collocation analysis, i.e. on discovering the 'meaning' of teacher(s) in news coverage by examining the words most frequently and closely associated with the two keywords. Firth (1957) is often quoted for his succinct reference to the importance of collocation, 'You shall know a lot about a word from the company it keeps,' and numerous studies (e.g. Stubbs 2002; Baker 2006; Lind and Salo 2002; Pudrovska and Ferree 2004) have shown the significant power and robustness of corpus linguistic co-word or collocation analysis as a key to discovering patterns of association and meaning, which become visible only through the systematic analysis of large bodies of text. An important component of the lexical analysis focuses on the types of discourses invoked through the use of particular words and metaphors (e.g. a discourse of combat/conflict).

The principal analytical tool used in this analysis was the computer programme Concordance (Watt 2002), which allows the production of a concordance (a full list, arranged either alphabetically or by frequency, of each individual word in the text), a listing of each word in its immediate context (also sometimes referred to as a keyword-in-context view), and the analysis of collocations (a listing of the words – and their frequency – appearing immediately to the left or to the right of selected keywords).

The sample analysed here comprises the headlines from newspaper coverage of teachers and education during selected years from 1991 through 2005. All newspaper articles were sampled from the full-text database Lexis/Nexis. Articles were selected for the sample if they included one or more variations on the word-stem 'teach' or the word-stem 'educat' in either the headline or the first paragraph of the article.

For the years 2003 and 2005, the sample comprises all coverage of teachers and education in 17 national daily and Sunday newspapers and 5 regional newspapers,[1] sampled as every eighth day from 14 March–15 September in 2003 and again in 2005 (48 days in total).

For the period 1991 to 2002, sampling was restricted to those newspapers available in electronic form for the full period, namely *The Financial Times, The Guardian, The Observer, The Independent, The Independent on Sunday, The Times* and *The Sunday Times*. The sampling combined the purposive sampling of three year-clusters (1991–93 (three years), 1996–98 (three years) and 2001–02 (two years)) with systematic random sampling (using a sampling interval of 15 days) within these. The systematic sampling from the selected eight years produced 194 sampling dates. After removing all articles, which were not principally about teachers or education, the total number of headlines used in the present analysis was 5419 (comprising 1717 headlines from 2003/2005 and 3702 headlines from the three selected year-clusters from 1991–2002). The emphasis in the present analysis is on changes over time in news portrayal of teachers, rather than on differences across types of newspaper.

The image of teachers in newspaper headlines, 1991–2005

Teacher/teachers collocates 1991–2005

An indication of the overall 'image' of teachers, as they are represented or portrayed in newspaper headlines, comes from a collocation-analysis, that is, an analysis of the words most frequently occurring together with the two key-words 'teacher' and 'teachers'. Table 1 below shows the top most frequently occurring meaning-carrying words appearing within two words either side of the word 'teacher' or the word 'teachers'. The table only lists meaning-carrying collocates of 'teacher(s)' and excludes the most common articles (a, an, the) and verbs (is, are, etc.), as well as numbers and prepositions.

The very considerable emphasis on teachers involved in court cases and/or as victims or perpetrators of (sexual) misconduct and violence is clearly signalled through the extraordinarily frequent collocates jail/jailed, air-gun/gun, rape/raped and sex, and the further prominence of the collocates murder/murdered, seduced, attack/attacked/attacks, killed and porn. As simple word-associations, these collocates - together with a further generally negative set comprising 'sacked/sacking', 'loses', 'appeal', 'fears', 'charge/charged', 'face/facing' (i.e. it is rare for the

Table 1. Collocations of TEACHER and TEACHERS in all headlines (significant words within 2 words either side of Teacher or Teachers).

TEACHER collocates	N	TEACHERS collocates	N
Jail (12), jailed (15)	27	Head	9
Training (14) trainee (1)	15	Pay	9
Air-gun (8), gun (2)	10	Union (6), unions (3)	9
Head	9	School (1), schools (7)	8
Rape (6), raped (2)	8	Strike (7), striking (1)	8
Union (1), Unions (6),	8	Call (5), calls (2)	7
Super-union (1)		Train (2), trained (1), trainee (1),	7
Favourite	7	trainers (2), training (2)	
Sex	7	New	6
Dance (4), danced (1), dancer (1)	6	Conference (2), conferences (3)	5
Murder (5), murdered (1)	6	Demand	5
Sacked (5), sacking (1)	6	Need (4), needed (1)	5
Seduced	6	Some	5
Appeal	5	Vote	5
Face (1), faces (2), facing (2)	5	Accuse (1), accused (3)	4
Job	5	Action	4
Loses	5	Attack (1), attacks (3)	4
PE	5	Class (3), classroom (1)	4
Attack (1), attacked (1), attacks (2)	4	Cut (3), cuts (1)	4
Boy (3), boys (1)	4	Do	4
Fears	4	Doctors	4
Justice	4	English	4
Killed	4	Fear (1), fears (3)	4
Pet	4	Get (3), gets (1)	4
Case	3	Give (2), given (2)	4
Charge (1), charged (2)	3	Inner-city	4
Crisis	3	Pupil (2), pupils (2)	4
Drive (1, verb), driven (2)	3	Reject (3), rejects (1)	4
Education	3	Threaten (3), threatens (1)	4
Held	3	Time	4
Mathematics (1), maths (2)	3	Want	4
Porn	3	Blame (2), blamed (1)	3
Pupil (2), pupils (1)	3	Go	3
Row	3	Hour (1), hours (2)	3
Shortage (2), shortages (1)	3	Just	3
Spill	3	Leader	3
Talk (2), talks (1)	3	Oppose	3
Top ('top 1500' and 'top school')	3	Rise (2), rises (1)	3
		Should	3

*Frequent collocates like BRIEF, LETTER and EDUCATION are not included as they generally appear as type-of-article identifiers only.

verb 'face/facing' to be used in conjunction with something positive), 'crisis', 'driven' and 'row' – convey an image of teachers in trouble (because of their conduct) or 'under siege' in terms of the violence committed against them or the pressures on them.

Positive collocations include the prominent headline-occurrence of the phrase 'My *favourite* teacher', which stems from a celebrities-praise-their-favourite-teacher series run by *The Guardian* in 1997. Teacher-training, the second most prominent co-occurrence, is not by itself either necessarily negative or positive, but indicates the prominent political and news-interest in reform and enhancement of the training of teachers.

While clearly showing the most prominent associations in news-headline referencing of teachers, this kind of analysis is easily skewed by a few prominently reported specific cases: thus the frequent collocation 'airgun teacher' relates to a single, but much covered, story. 'Dance teacher' likewise relates to the reporting of a single story concerning a female dance teacher who had a sexual relationship with one of her under-age pupils. The collocation 'favourite teacher' falls into a similar category, a single newspaper using this phrase in a celebrity-focused series.

The most frequent collocates of the plural form 'teachers' are notable for the general image which they convey of teachers as a union-organised body (with particular unions/associations for 'head teachers'), making claims regarding pay and conditions (e.g. 'hours') and threatening strike action. The headlines focus on organised confrontation, on head teachers' and other teachers' Union-related 'strike'/'pay'/'action' and 'calls', threats, 'demands', rejection, 'votes' – at union 'conferences'.

Changing images of teachers, 1991–2005

The portrayal of teachers changed considerably over this period. The most noticeable change between the headlines of 1991–93 and those of 1996–98 is a syntactic change in the position of teacher(s) from an almost exclusive position as object/target of government and other actions to a much more active position as the subject/agent of various actions.

In the 1991–93 headlines education secretary Patten 'defies' and 'threatens' teachers, a teacher is 'told', the 'Minister tries to head off teachers dispute', teachers are taught a lesson ('The lesson that the Tories have taught teachers'), 'Teachers at fee-paying schools [are] hit by job losses' or 'Teachers [are] blocked in effort to offer range of subjects', 'Teachers put to test', 'Extremist teachers [are] curbed', 'Patten proposes one-year college courses to train mature students as infant teachers', 'Schools to train teachers'. Amidst the prominent teachers-as-object references only a few headlines portrayed teachers in the subject/agency role of doing something: 'Teachers hold to defiant line', 'Teachers oppose ... [truancy tables/training proposal]' and 'Teacher won't be dismissed'.

By 1996–1998, teachers are very predominantly portrayed as subjects and in an active role: here, teachers variously 'have grave doubts', 'prepare to strike', 'say', 'beat clampdown', 'find it harder', 'savage reading report', 'demand', 'accuse Shephard', 'boo', 'threaten', 'object', are 'enraged', 'reject', 'ask' etc. Unlike the 1991–93 headlines, there are very few occurrences of teachers as objects/targets, although such sentence constructions do of course still occur: e.g. 'Boy, 12, attacks teacher', 'Teacher jailed for armed robbery', 'Shephard expels scruffy teachers from classroom' and 'Shephard seeks to raise hurdle for new teachers'.

The 'teacher'-headlines of the 2001–02 year-cluster are similar to those of the 1996–98 year-cluster in that teachers – both as individuals and as a group/profession – continue to be portrayed predominantly in a subject – rather than an object – position in sentence-structures. There is thus a clear and seemingly lasting change from the teachers-as-object position characteristic of the headlines of the early 1990s to a teachers-as-subject/agency representation in the latter half of the 1990s and early

2000s. This signals a change in the public image and representation of teachers, from a position of less respect and status in the sense that we are told what is done to/said about teachers to one where teachers are portrayed/reported in the subject/agent position – with the added credibility and legitimacy associated with such a position; in other words, teachers are given a 'voice' and what is reported is predominantly what teachers say/demand/ask for/call for/claim/do etc.

With very few exceptions the 'teacher' headlines of 1991–93 are 'problem' or 'confrontation' news stories. There are few distinctly 'good/positive' news stories, exceptions being: 'Classroom fit for modern teacher', 'Teacher prize launched', 'Teacher of the Year', 'Further education for better teachers'. Much more commonly headlines focus on resource/pay/employment-problems and highlight conflict/ disputes between teachers/teacher-unions and government: e.g 'Teacher unions attack Clarke for outrageous slur on profession', 'Teacher union ready to give Patten a lesson', 'Minister tries to head off teachers dispute', – 'Tory unease as Patten defies teachers over tests boycott', 'Teachers hold to defiant line', 'Teachers leader appeals for truce', 'Patten threatens teachers on tests', 'Extremist teachers curbed', 'Warning of cut in teacher numbers', 'Teacher redundancies warning', 'Teachers' pay rises will cost jobs and materials' and 'teachers ... hit by job losses'.

The language used is predominantly the language of crisis, violence, conflict and combat with words such as 'crisis', 'action', 'strike', 'dispute', 'launch offensive', 'assault', 'blocked', 'rule by diktat', 'truce', 'threatens', 'oppose', 'boycott', 'defiant' and 'defies'. While the lexicon of crisis and conflict continues to be prevalent throughout the period examined, the image of teachers becomes much less one-dimensional both in the 1996–98 and in the 2001–02 year-clusters. There is a noticeable shift in the 2001–02 headlines, particularly compared to the 1991–93 headlines, but also to a lesser extent compared with the 1996–98 headlines, towards a more diverse range of issues and towards an openly supportive recognition of the problems facing teachers and the profession. Thus two Leader/editorial headlines explicitly support calls for more teachers and better pay:

- The best way to improve school standards is to employ more teachers
- More from Morris: but teachers are still underpaid

Where the 1991–93 headlines focus mainly on problems of discipline/violence in schools, on pay, on standards and on 'bad' teachers in a range of misconduct or criminal cases, the 1996–98 headlines and particularly the 2001–02 headlines give considerable emphasis – in addition to the court-case and misconduct reporting – to pensions, working hours and workloads, teacher training, recruitment, teacher shortages and 'attractive' features of a teaching career. Where the 1991–93 and 1996–98 year-cluster headlines highlighted concerns about teacher training in terms of teachers' and others' concerns about dilution of standards and de-professionalisation, the 2001–02 headlines portray 'training' in an almost promotional language. Thus, terms like 'job satisfaction', 'incentive', 'attractive', 'attracted', 'accessible', and 'help' (to teachers), appear in the 2001–02 headlines but less frequently, or not at all, in those of the earlier year-clusters.

While there is little overtly negative or directly derogatory or disparaging comment on teachers (with the exception of headlines about teachers jailed or sentenced for criminal behaviour of various sorts) in any of the year-clusters, the tone of the 2001–02 headlines is noticeably more sympathetic to teachers than the

1991–93 headlines. The tone cannot be separated from the change in object/subject-position commented on above, but it extends further than this in at least two ways: (1) through affording 'news space' to the cataloguing of a wide range of issues/problems facing the teaching profession, and (2) through the tone of reporting which generally conveys acknowledgement and recognition by the newspapers that these issues or problems are genuine and legitimate (in contrast to coverage which would imply that teachers were forever whinging or were militant, extremist, obstinate, regressive, unreasonable etc.).

Repeated news attention is thus given, in the 2001–02 headlines in particular, to the (implied: unacceptable or difficult) general plight of teachers as a beleaguered profession, reflected in the many headlines cataloguing the range of problems associated with teaching and the teaching profession. The problems include, inter alia, teacher shortages/recruitment/retention, pay (which is either recognised by the headlines as still being too low per se or described as such in reports which focus on the mismatch between teachers' pay and the cost of housing/living in parts of the country, notably London), workloads and hours, problems of discipline and violence, lack of appropriate powers to exclude disruptive pupils and enforce discipline, intimidation by parents, stress, safety and teacher liability on school outings, pension shortfalls, etc.

Not only are these issues/problems given prominence on the news agenda, but in addition the tone of coverage is one of recognition that they are genuine problems, and one of sympathy and support:

- Analysis: teacher's hours – the formula for a rise in school standards: lighter workload = greater recruitment.
- Analysis: teacher's hours – case study Gill Bland, primary school teacher.
- Teacher training drive to lift results: Minister says targets will be hit next year.
- Pay package wins backing of Scots teachers.
- Fast-track inquiry plan for accused teachers.
- Blunkett to offer help for teachers accused of abuse.
- State teachers 'should share in school profits'.
- Business: Teacher Training: Opening up the school doors: Amid the worst shortage of teachers in 20 years, training is becoming more accessible.
- Teachers hit by bad advice on pensions.
- Teachers' stress and long hours.
- Head teachers warn over school violence.
- Teaching lures 'dissatisfied' recruits from private sector; schools more than half the people becoming teachers are over 30 as the security, hours and job satisfaction prove increasingly attractive.

The 2003–05 headlines mirror to a large extent those of 2001–2002 in terms of both the range of issues and in terms of the image and generally sympathetic tone conveyed. Particularly interesting, when comparing with headlines of the early 1990s, is the almost complete absence of references conveying the notion that teachers are being ordered, told or commanded to do this or that – and associated with this absence, an absence of headlines implying that teachers are being set unreasonable goals by government. As noted in relation to headlines from the 1996–98 and 2001–02 year-clusters, there is also a marked predominance of 'teachers' in the grammatical position as sentence subject/agent rather than in the object-position prevalent in the headlines of the early 1990s. In 2003–05 teachers variously 'tell', 'demand', 'seek', 'may', 'need', 'want', 'vote', 'are', 'call for', 'threaten', 'attack' etc. The emphasis then is on articulating teachers' voices or perspectives, with the credibility and authority that this grammatical position affords over the grammatical object-position.

Although the lexicon of combat, crisis and conflict continues to be present, there is less headline-reference to or linguistic emphasis on direct confrontation between teachers and government. Where headlines of earlier year-clusters often refer to clashes/conflict between teachers/teacher-unions and Government (frequently in the form of direct reference to the Secretary of State for Education, government ministers or the Department for Education and Skills) and occasionally to clashes/ conflict between teachers and the political opposition, there are relatively and comparatively few of these types of 'confrontation'-references in the 2003/2005 headlines.

Continuing the trend identified in the 2001–02 headlines, the headlines of 2003–05 predominantly highlight the range of problems facing teachers, in a form which generally conveys teachers' own perspective, is overtly laudatory, or affords legitimacy and/or sympathy in relation to their situation or plight:

- Teachers' zeal gets results.
- Education: 'Teachers at difficult schools should be paid as much as they are at Eton'.
- The big issues: Classroom chaos: Time for teachers to just say no.
- Education: Teach: Deep end: Diary of a primary teacher.
- Education: Opinion: Creative teachers should be positively encouraged, not made to toe the line.
- Leading article: The teachers are right: Tests are no substitute for education.

As in previous year-clusters, the 2003–2005 headlines contain a large number of references to individual teachers in the context of misconduct, violence, discipline, abuse, and sex-related cases of various sorts. While at a simple word-association level these clearly contribute to a negative image of individual teachers, with perhaps unavoidable extensions to the profession as such, such headlines are, however, not exclusively anti-teachers or negative. Thus, a large number of the 'violence, crime, jail'-related headlines referencing teachers in the 2003–2005 quality newspaper headlines point to the unreasonable pressures on teachers, problems of discipline/ lack of respect, threats and violence against teachers, inadequate legal and other backing for teachers to enable them to defend themselves or to enable them to enforce order and discipline in schools, etc. The perspective is one which is critical of the wider context and system within which teachers are forced to operate, not of the teachers themselves. The tone of these headlines is one which supports the 'case' of teachers. Numerous headlines in the 2005 sample thus related to a single story regarding a teacher's use of an airgun:

- Teacher gets six months for air pistol clash with 'vandals'.
- Six months for teacher who took on 'yobbos'.
- Teacher who fired air gun at 'vandals' is sent to jail.
- Air gun teacher sacked by school.
- Air-gun teacher loses job appeal.

While the newspaper headlines are careful to appropriately indicate, with quotation marks, that the labels 'vandals' and 'yobbos' are from the court evidence and not their terms, the message that is clearly communicated is that the teacher in question reacted in response to unacceptable taunting and pressure, and was unduly harshly punished by both a jail-sentence and by being sacked from her job.

The headline identifier 'teacher', and later the nominalization 'air-gun teacher', is notable for the fact that the person in question is consistently identified by her profession, as a teacher, even though the vandalism, taunting and indeed the air-gun incident itself took place near her home and was unrelated to her place of work or to her profession. The consistent use of the identifier 'teacher' is thus an important part of the way that the newspapers – without using language or descriptors that could be regarded as biased or value-laden – build up a 'frame' and perspective to signal whether the person's behaviour was justified and appropriately dealt with by, in this case, the legal system. The identifier 'teacher' is used to convey the normal qualities associated with this profession, namely as someone who is respectable, reasonable and – as the text beyond the headlines stresses in more detail - doing a valuable and caring job (e.g. 'Mrs Walker, a teacher at New Park High School in Eccles, Salford, a special school for children with behavioural problems . . .' *The Independent*, 17 May 2005).

These positive associations with the label 'teacher' are further emphasised by the juxtaposition with the negative labels 'vandals' and 'yobbos'. The larger news-study, described briefly earlier, found that the label 'teacher' often appears as an identifier in stories unrelated to teaching, education or the profession as such and is used essentially to convey, in shorthand fashion, the positive cultural values and characteristics associated with the teaching profession. There are thus no instances in this analysis of the label 'teacher' ever being used – on its own – as a negative identifier. The 'air-gun teacher' headlines confirm this general argument in the sense that the primary headline identification of the person involved is through her professional label as a 'teacher' (as opposed to other possible identifiers that could have been used: e.g. 'mother', '47-year-old', 'Urmston resident', etc.), even though the incident itself seemed unrelated to both the place and nature of her work as a teacher. 'Teacher' is used as part of the newspapers' building of a character-profile (together with age, relationships (partner, son, etc), place of living and place of incident) and this is further cemented through the juxtaposition with the negative labels used in relation to her accusers.

While many headlines focus on teachers who have unlawful sexual relationships with (underage) pupils in their charge, and while there is certainly media coverage of bad teachers who commit violence or other criminal offences, there is also much coverage, particularly in the post-2000 headlines, stressing that teachers are too easily and often wrongfully accused, that they are victims of violence – and murder in some cases – battling against a rising tide of indiscipline, disruptive behaviour, harassment from pupils as well as parents etc.

Summary and conclusions

News coverage of teachers and education features prominently in both national and regional newspapers. Newspapers are thus an important public arena for definitions of what the key issues, challenges and tasks facing education and teachers are, as well as potentially a key source of public definitions of the identity and status of teachers. While it would be foolhardy to think of the role of news-definitions of teachers and education in terms of 'direct impact' on political, public or teachers' own perceptions of the status of teachers, the analysis presented here shows the reservoir of public images from which such perceptions may draw. The study's retrospective analysis of the portrayal of teachers from 1991 to 2005 shows a considerable and important change from a largely negative to a largely positive portrayal of teachers.

There was much explicitly positive or supportive reporting of teachers, increasingly so towards the latter end of the 1990s and through 2005, and not infrequently casting teachers as 'heroically' fighting against extraordinary outside pressures on them, the education system and on students. The identifier 'teacher' itself was shown to carry powerful positive connotations. While much coverage focused on confrontation between teacher unions and government or government related institutions, there was markedly less emphasis on confrontation – and concomitantly more emphasis on support and help to teachers – in the most recent period.

The misconduct of individual 'bad' teachers was highly newsworthy and consequently figured prominently in the headlines, but it was extremely rare to find headlines which showed teachers – as a body of professionals – as anything other than dedicated and committed professionals struggling against a broad range of serious problems and pressures. Earlier news coverage of the teacher bashing mould (Ball 1990, Wallace 1993, Woods et al. 1997) has given way to a more supportive and less confrontational style of reporting, which gives teachers a prominent voice and recognises, as genuine, the problems and pressures faced by teachers.

Methodologically, the analysis sought to combine the recognised analytical strengths of critical discourse analysis (particularly its twin focus on lexical choice and syntactical structures) with the computer-assisted tools and strengths of corpus linguistics. The latter concerned particularly the ability to reliably identify the occurrence and context of selected key-words in large and representative bodies of text, as well as the ability to systematically make transparent for analysis important changes over time. The tracking of changes in words associated with the keyword 'teacher(s)' (collocation analysis) and the ability (with the help of concordance software) to view all occurrences of the keywords in their immediate context combined to systematically reveal important lexical and syntactical shifts, over the period analysed here, in the way teachers are referred to and characterised in newspaper discourse. The mapping of such shifts in news coverage in turn provides a context for understanding important changes in public and political – as well as teachers' own – perception of the status and condition of teachers.

In summary, the study showed that the image of teachers and the teaching profession changed and improved considerably between the early 1990s and 2005. While there was, due to the intrinsic news-value of such stories, a great deal of headline coverage of 'bad' individual teachers in sexual and other misconduct cases, teachers – as a professional body – were increasingly portrayed in a way which implied respectability and esteem, which afforded recognition to their claims, and which recognised their plight and (sometimes) beleaguered situation as a genuine problem requiring political action.

Note

1. **National quality newspapers**: *The Guardian* and *The Observer, The Times* and *The Sunday Times, The Independent* and *The Independent on Sunday, The Daily Telegraph* and *The Sunday Telegraph, The Financial Times*. **National popular newspapers**: *The Sun* and the *News of the World, The Mirror* and *The Sunday Mirror, The Express* and *The Sunday Express, The Daily Mail* and *The Mail on Sunday*. **Regional newspapers**: *The Birmingham*

Evening Mail (West Midlands), *The Leicester Mercury* (East Midlands), *The Newcastle Evening Chronicle* (North East), *The Yorkshire Evening Post* (Yorkshire and Humber), *The London Evening Standard* (London). The exclusion of newspapers specific to home countries other than England is acknowledged, and this 'bias' should be borne in mind in relation to questions about the potential distinctiveness of media coverage of teachers and education within the different countries of Britain.

References

Baker, P. 2006. *Using corpora in discourse analysis.* London: Continuum International Publishing Group Ltd.

Baker, P., and T. McEnery. 2005. A corpus-based approach to discourses of refugees and asylum seekers in UN and newspaper texts. *Journal of Language and Politics* 4, no. 2: 197–226.

Ball, S.J. 1990. *Politics and policy making in education: Explorations in policy sociology.* London: Routledge.

Biber, D., S. Conrad, and R. Reppen. 1998. *Corpus linguistics: Investigating language structure and use.* Cambridge: Cambridge University Press.

Blackmore, J., and P. Thomson. 2004. Just 'good and bad news'? Disciplinary imaginaries of head teachers in Australian and English print media. *Journal of Education Policy* 19, no. 3: 301–20.

Cunningham, P. 1992. Teachers' professional image and the press 1950–1990. *History of Education* 21, no. 1: 37–56.

Dalton, M.M. 2003. *The Hollywood curriculum.* Rev. ed. New York: P. Lang.

Ellismore, S. 2005. *Carry on teachers! Representations of the teaching profession in screen culture.* Stoke on Trent: Trentham Books Ltd.

Entman, R.M. 1993. Framing: Toward clarification of a fractured paradigm. *Journal of Communication* 43, no. 4: 51–8.

Fairclough, N. 2003. *Analysing discourse: Textual analysis for social research.* London: Routledge.

Firth, J.R. 1957. *Papers in linguistics 1934–1951.* London: Oxford University Press.

Fowler, R. 1991. *Language in the news: Discourse and ideology in the press.* London: Routledge.

Franklin, B. 1998. *Hard pressed: National newspaper reporting of social work and social services.* Sutton: Community Care.

Franklin, B., ed. 1999. *Social policy, the media and misrepresentation.* London: Routledge.

Gamson, W. 1985. Goffman's legacy to political sociology. *Theory and Society* 14, no. 5: 605–22.

Hargreaves, L., M. Cunningham, A. Hansen, D. McIntyre, C. Oliver, and T. Pell. 2007. *The Status of teachers and the teaching profession in England: Views from inside and outside the profession: Final report of the teacher status project* (Research Report RR831A). London: Department for Education and Skills.

Hilgartner, S., and C.L. Bosk. 1988. The rise and fall of social problems: A public arenas model. *American Journal of Sociology* 94, no. 1: 53–78.

Hodge, R., and G. Kress. 1993. *Language as ideology.* 2nd ed. London: Routledge.

Lacey, C., and D. Longman. 1997. *The press as public educator: Cultures of understanding, cultures of ignorance.* Luton: University of Luton Press.

Lind, R.A., and C. Salo. 2002. The framing of feminists and feminism in news and public affairs programs in US electronic media. *Journal of Communication* 52, no. 1: 211–28.

Maeroff, G.I., ed. 1998. *Imaging education: The media and schools in America.* Teachers College Press.

McCombs, M. 2004. *Setting the agenda: The mass media and public opinion.* Cambridge: Polity.

Pudrovska, T., and M.M. Ferree. 2004. Global activism in 'virtual space': The european women's lobby in the network of transnational women's NGOs on the web. *Social Politics* 11, no. 1: 117–43.

Reese, S.D. 2001. Prologue – Framing public life: A bridging model for media research. In *Framing public life: Perspectives on media and our understanding of the social world*, ed. S.D. Reese, O.H. Gandy, and A.E. Grant, 7–31. Mahwah, NJ: Lawrence Erlbaum Associates.

Stubbs, M. 1996. *Text and corpus analysis: Computer assisted studies of language and culture.* Oxford: Blackwell Publishers.

Stubbs, M. 2002. *Words and phrases: Corpus studies of lexical semantics.* Oxford; Malden, MA: Blackwell.

Wallace, M. 1993. Discourse of derision: The role of mass media within the education policy process. *Journal of Education Policy* 8, no. 4: 321–37.

Watt, R.J.C. 2002. *Concordance: Manual for version 3.0.* Dundee: University of Dundee.

Wiklund, M. 2003. The making of the good teacher in Swedish media debates – Discursive constructions of teachers in Dagens Nyheter 1982–2002. Paper presented at the European Conference on Educational Research, University of Hamburg, September 17–20, 2003.

Woods, P., B. Jeffrey, G. Troman, and M. Boyle. 1997. *Restructuring schools, reconstructing teachers: Responding to change in the primary school.* Buckingham: Open University Press.

Zaller, J.R. 1992. *The nature and origins of mass opinion.* New York: Cambridge University Press.

Missing out? Challenges to hearing the views of all children on the barriers and supports to learning

Jill Porter

Department of Education, University of Bath, UK

Children's views are essential to enabling schools to fulfil their duties under the Special Educational Needs and Disability Act 2001 and create inclusive learning environments. Arguably children are the best source of information about the ways in which schools support their learning and what barriers they encounter. Accessing this requires a deeper level of reflection than simply asking what children find difficult. It is also a challenge to ensure that the views of all children contribute including those who find communication difficult. Development work in five schools is drawn on to analyse the ways in which teachers used suggestions for three interview activities. The data reveals the strengths and limitations of different ways of supporting the communication process.

Introduction

In recent years there has been a burgeoning interest in the views of children particularly with respect to bringing about changes in teaching and learning. The Special Educational Needs (SEN) and Disability Act (2001) amended the Disability Discrimination Act (DDA) (1995) and reinforced the importance of ensuring that all children contribute their views to the process of improving teaching and learning (DfES 2006). Schools have been required to draw up a Disability Equality Scheme setting out their plans to promote equality with active participation of people with a disability, including staff, parents and children. This includes pupils who might be described as difficult to communicate with, either due to language, communication or learning difficulties (LD) or because of social, emotional and behavioural difficulties (SEBD). It challenges schools to extend their good practices beyond selected groups of children to those who might be considered harder to reach.

Recent research suggests that although schools and local authorities may have near complete registers of children with SEN, their data on children with a disability is far more patchy (Porter et al. 2008; Mooney, Owen, and Statham 2008). A national survey found that just under a third of the children who met the DDA criteria did not have an SEN and in a number of cases these children were unknown to school (Porter et al. 2008). Schools may therefore be uncertain about which additional children have a disability and consequently unaware of some of the difficulties their pupils face and the ways in which they cope with them.

Guidance on approaches to 'interviewing' children with a disability comes from a number of different investigative and evidential sources (Lewis and Porter 2007). These draw on research using a range of both familiar methods (focus groups, questionnaires and individual conversations) as well as novel methods that include the use of different stimulus material (e.g. video clips, photographs, posters, stories, letters) and activities (e.g. mind mapping, drawing, keeping a diary). These methods have been used in: research on forensic and clinical work; the evaluation of curricula and provision of services; researching children's cognitive understanding; and developing participatory approaches involving research with children and young people with a disability. Given the range of circumstances and the different underlying values and assumptions it is not surprising that some of this guidance can be contradictory, making it important for the user to be open and reflective about work in their own setting (Lambert 2008). This guidance will be reviewed to reflect on the data arising from development work with mainstream and special schools.

Linguistic demands of questioning children

Studies based on an analysis of forensic interviews have made an important contribution to guidance with a focus on the reliability and validity of children's responses. Some of the research has been naturalistic field work (e.g. Cederburg et al. 2000; Lamb and Fauchier 2001) and others simulated studies (e.g. Krahenbuhl and Blades 2006; Bruck, Ceci, and Hembrooke 2002; Orbach and Lamb 2001) designed to inform judicial interviewing. These provide unusual circumstances as often the child is subject to repeated questioning, being asked either the same or similar questions, with less emphasis on opinion and more on accuracy of reporting. However, like the target group in our development project, they may be being asked about circumstances that make them emotionally uncomfortable. In particular such research has supported the use of open questions with children which are likely to give accurate information and less likely to produce contradictory statements; however they are also less likely to produce complete answers (Lamb and Fauchier 2001). Open prompts ('tell me more about that?') are then a good response. In contrast option-posing questions (often used with the least articulate) together with suggestive or leading questions are much more likely to produce inaccurate responses. Repeating a question leads to a decrease in accuracy (Krahenbuhl and Blades 2006). This is particularly the case for questions that are unanswerable, which younger children will try and answer rather than replying that they do not know, although by the age of seven children are more likely to indicate their uncertainty in their response (Hughes and Grieve 1980). A similar finding occurs but to a slightly lesser degree with responses that require an opinion. Quite reasonably children appear to assume that adults ask them questions for which they should know the answer and, if adults are not happy with the one they receive then they ask again.

This research provides useful guidance for interviewing many children but as we shall see provides an insight into the difficulties faced when children are less articulate. It has been challenged by Booth and Booth (1996) who write about the place of closed questions and the importance of listening to silence. There is also a popular account in the literature of the tendency of people with learning difficulties to acquiesce (or say yes) (Finlay and Lyons 2002) with explanations of their greater suggestibility or desire to please. This characteristic is not however specific to people with special needs, it also happens when children do not have an opinion, or they have been asked a complex or unanswerable question. Research also illustrates the ways in which children and young people with learning difficulties may be more likely to say they like [something] rather than dislike providing views that sometimes contradict the opinions and observations of others (Germain 2005; Wright 2008). This, however, is also reflected in research with young children. Fritzley and Lee (2003) found that given a yes/no question, two year olds showed a consistent bias towards saying 'yes' whereas four and five year olds showed no such response bias and three year olds were mixed, and described as being in a stage of developmental transition. Their analysis gives some interesting suggestions of why children may find a particular response more salient than another, including that it may be seen as an effective way to stop adults questioning.

Cognitive demands of questioning children

The emphasis in guidance is often on linguistic aspects but children's cognitive skills also play an important role, in particular memory as children are less likely to be interviewed about events as they happen. It is therefore important to consider the time lag between events and being asked about views, and to recognize that the cognitive demands vary between being asked to describe an event that has just happened, to anticipate something that will shortly happen and to make a longer term prediction (Dockrell 2004). Much research with young children and those with learning difficulties uses stimulus material, (often photographs) to prompt the child, drawing on our knowledge of the differential ease of recognition over recall. There is however a body of research reviewed by Dockrell (2004) that indicates how hard it may be to recall emotions accurately with a tendency to overstate an initial emotional reaction if the event has been successfully responded to.

It is also important to recognize the cognitive demands of ensuring that the methods and approach adopted make it clear to the child that disclosure is voluntary. Pupils with SEN are particularly vulnerable to being included in research without their consent not least because the skills required. Understanding the information about an unfamiliar event, weighing up the pros and cons through predicting what the experience will be like and communicating that choice, may well be ones that the child struggles with (Cameron and Murphy 2006). There is consistent agreement that consent should be an on-going process. As individuals come to understand through experience what is involved, they should be given the option of stopping the activity (Curtis et al. 2004; Porter and Lacey 2005; Cameron and Murphy 2006). Others have also argued that children might be given more choice about the type of activities consent will involve and with whom they would like to work (Punch 2002).

The study

This contribution draws on research undertaken on behalf of the Department for Children, Schools and Families (DCSF) to develop tools and activities through which schools could fulfil their obligations under the Disability Equality Duty and collect the views of *all* children on the barriers and supports to learning. It uses data collected during the development phase of the project to illustrate the methodological challenges encountered and to reflect on the implications for future practice. It does so recognizing the importance, as others have, that we do not simply airbrush our data (Curtis et al. 2004) but recognize the uncertainties and difficulties we face in fulfilling our duties.

Eleven schools were involved in this phase of the project including special schools for children with learning difficulties and for children with social emotional and behavioural difficulties, three secondary schools, one first school and four primary schools. The focus was pupils in years R, three and seven. The schools selected the tools they wished to pilot with their choice determined partly by the appropriateness of the tools for the pupils but also by pragmatic considerations of time and organisation. Teachers in mainstream were asked to use the tools with children with and without a disability. The use of the tools was observed wherever possible by a researcher. An analysis is provided of observations carried out in a first school, two primary schools and two special schools as they tried out activities drawing on guidance on the following three methods:

(i) Talking Mats: This is a symbol led system developed to enable people with learning disabilities to engage in decision-making around important issues in their lives (Cameron and Murphy 2002). It is particularly well suited to using with individuals who have limited formal systems of communication, although it does assume that individuals have an understanding of representation i.e. that a symbol or picture or a photograph is representative of the thing it depicts. Using this material, a facilitator asks children to indicate their like or dislike for particular activities and contexts for learning by placing personalised photographs alongside a symbol representation of like, dislike and a middle position of 'so-so'.

(ii) Structured Interviews: These were designed to be undertaken either individually or in a small group and explored children's favourite things about school, as well as those aspects they did not like doing, and asked what would make these activities easier. During the course of this pilot we also looked at a symbol based version being used in school which did not quite match our questions but provided insights into the range of support required by pupils and the guidance needed for staff.

(iii) Point to Point: This tool is based around counselling techniques and provides a concrete approach focusing on specific events that the child identifies as good or bad. Pupils represent these events with a mark on paper and position themselves on a visual scale, drawing a line between the best and worst events indicating where they feel they are today. This activity provides a vehicle for then exploring the barriers that contributed to the worst event and the positive supports that contributed to the best.

Making the activity meaningful

An important part of making the questions meaningful was to explain at the outset why the children were being asked about their experiences. One teacher very explicitly introduced the idea of research stating that if teachers know what makes a good or a bad day then they can make things better – explaining that as a teacher he is trained to think how to do it better and how to make it more interesting. Another teacher recalled. 'Do you remember assembly – a lady came in and gave us an award. . .? [There are still] lots of things we could be better at; how we could improve things, [There is] no right and wrong answer. We're interested in what you feel, not what teachers feel or parents but about what you guys feel.' In setting out the context, pupils were told how valued their views were and that they would change aspects of provision. Children need to feel staff genuinely want to hear their views and to act on them, that it's not a 'window-dressing' exercise (Stafford et al. 2003).

A number of additional strategies were used to convey this message including teachers sharing their own experiences or that of their offspring: one teacher spoke about his best day being when his first child was born; another of winning a rowing regatta and how he was helped by his family who gave him the money to go. The worst day for him was being disqualified for ramming a boat and loosing three races in a day. These were not examples that children would really identify with, lessening the chance of children making duplicate responses. Another teacher spoke about the struggle their child had learning to read. The examples contributed to an ethos of recognizing that everyone experiences difficulties of some kind, thus helping to create an atmosphere of trust. Other researchers investigating sensitive issues have suggested that it is useful for researchers to decide in advance which experiences to divulge (Curtis et al. 2004). It is important to recognize that there is a difference between experiencing ongoing difficulties and ones that are event specific. In providing models teachers give signals that potentially constrain what is viewed as being acceptable to say. Reference to valuing individual differences as well as 'Think(ing) for yourselves' are important.

Our observations suggested that in some settings children were being asked about their views in a way that had not been the focus of an activity before. This creates uncertainties about the nature of the activity and the expectations of adults, as well of course as being asked to reflect in a way that they might not have experienced before. Children therefore needed support in this and, in addition to providing exemplars and models, some staff gave clear guidelines:

> At some point children will think they need to tell me what Mr S should hear. This is not so – just be honest. . . Got to be honest, if it's a level of criticism you are free to say so, you have a responsibility to be honest.

Another said 'As long as it's true you are fine'.

Where it was a paired or group activity it was important to set ground rules and these included:

- Listen to each other.
- No put downs like in Circle Time.
- Recognize that we all have different ideas about what helps and what gets in the way.
- It's really important that everyone gets a say.

Finding the right questions

Finding the right language to use (Punch 2002) and how to articulate abstract concepts about learning (Deed 2008) proved one of the central challenges. The transcript extracts below illustrate the difficulty of finding an appropriate way to ask about barriers and supports, to turn the argot of adults to that of children.

The following transcript extract is taken from a teacher working with two year three boys one of whom (Jim) has a statement for speech and language difficulties. It shows how a seemingly simple question can be difficult to convey:

Teacher:	Jim what do you like doing best?
Jim:	House-points.
Teacher:	How do you feel when you get house points?
Jim:	Good?
Teacher to Harry:	What do you like best?
Harry:	Lunch.
Teacher:	What actual eating or playing after?
Harry:	Playing after.

Having gone on to discuss the games they like playing and who they like playing with the teacher then changes the focus of the discussion hoping that this will lead to a more reflective conversation:

Teacher:	Why do children come to school?
Harry:	To learn.
Teacher:	Is that right?
Teacher:	Why do you think Jim its important to come to school?
Jim remains very quiet.	
Harry:	Because I like going to school. My favourite thing is numbers.
Teacher:	Jim what do you think you're really good at?
Jim:	Good work.

While for Harry the lead is taken up, Jim's level of communication makes this harder. Questions have to be asked directly as he does not volunteer responses. She tries again by rephrasing to lead the conversation back to her agenda and while this works with Harry it does not with Jim. She does however keep with fairly open questions and in part this reflects the fact that she does not know the children very well. This has the advantage that she is less likely to use previous knowledge to ask closed questions, and the children do not make the assumption that the questions are ones she already knows the answers to.

Most teachers began by asking children about their likes and dislikes, usually starting with the former but some set the tone from the outset of having to think hard before responding and limiting their answers to aspects of school: 'Think about a special time in school when it was a really good day'. In general children found it more difficult to talk about things they didn't like, things they found hard. One child said that it was embarrassing to talk about things that were difficult, a message that is reflected elsewhere in the literature (Woolfson et al. 2007). Staff posed a number of different questions:

- What at school do you find most difficult?
- What things make for a horrible day? Things you find hard.
- Think about the best and worst things in school, things that get in the way of or support learning.
- If you had a magic wand and wanted to change something you find difficult or tricky.

Again there were differences in the extent to which they accessed responses that would lead to discussions of barriers and supports:

Teacher:	Can you think of a time when things were sad at school, you felt low? [It is] hard thinking about times that weren't nice.
Malcolm:	When I jumped down the stairs and hurt my foot – I couldn't walk.
Teacher:	What don't you find easy, [that you're] not so good at, something you struggle with find a little bit tricky?
Silence.	
Teacher:	When you haven't felt happy?
Rose:	When I…had to eat lunch. When I can't talk when I'm learning.
Michael:	When I tripped up … football … fallen over and hurt self.

Asking about emotions may help the child locate events and asking about something that is 'tricky' suggests that there is a shared understanding that it might be difficult. It appears easier for children to talk about physical hurts. However those who had framed their questions from the beginning in the context of learning elicited more specific answers:

Teacher:	What do you find hard to do? What do you find tricky?
Tony:	Maths is tricky. I just don't understand.
Mark:	Behaving well in the classroom.
John:	Literacy. I get stuck for ideas in stories.
Claire:	Having to do everything so fast.
Greta:	I miss out on the good parts of lessons when I have to go and see people.

Although it may appear deceptively simple it takes some time to access children's thoughts and includes spending time talking about occasions which may bring bad memories for the child. Indeed one teacher felt that she was not sufficiently trained to encourage these conversations. Other staff moved rapidly over these aspects or ran out of time before they reached them but in the Social Emotional and Behavioral Difficulties (SEBD) school some of the teachers made more detailed and specific prompts:

- Which people help you in school?
- What things help the day go well?
- Which people at school make things difficult?
- What things at school make it your worst day?
- What does it take to improve your day?

These presented pupils with a direct indication of what types of information might help them to think about the issue. The school found these questions provided particularly enlightening information.

Supporting communication

For children with more significant disabilities the level of support needs to be greater. The following is taken from an observation of a special school assistant trying to interview Oliver in year 7 of a special school. She is using a structured set of questions that were part of a school designed questionnaire. The transcript illustrates the ways in which faced by a difficult task, the interviewer provides 'a supportive cradle' (Antaki, Young, and Finlay 2002). She rewords questions in a way that she feels is more likely to elicit a response, often referring to something that she explicitly knows. As a result the child eventually produces the 'right' answer and previous responses are forgotten. This illustrates the dangers of trying to change what is for the child an essentially unanswerable question into a kind of dialogue:

Questionnaire: Do you have friends at school?

Teaching Assistant:	Who's your friend Mrs … ?
Oliver:	Joyce, Jac.
Teaching Assistant:	Who do you run round the playground with?
Oliver:	Naomi.
Teaching Assistant:	So you have friends?
Oliver:	No.
Teaching Assistant:	Have you got friends at school?
Oliver:	No.
Teaching Assistant:	(asks again)
Oliver:	Yes.

(This was recorded by the member of staff as asking the question twice and answering Yes.)

The transcript reveals the tendency for her to repeat questions that have a surprising answer – in one sense this is a natural response to check for misunderstanding, however it can also suggest to the child that it was not the right answer. She asks the friend question three times – he should in her view be able to answer this. While this approach can be seen as shaping the child's answers, it also illustrates the ways in which the assistant tries to contextualise the questions to make them more meaningful to the child, more personalised, and more answerable. One of the challenges for her is to ensure that the conclusions she records are a reasonable representation.

Activities

Observations of the activities in schools revealed that given a choice and guidelines for different activities staff made these their own and often took elements from different activities. This creativity and making things fit for purpose was supported by the research team. However it proved a learning experience as some activities lost their focus. The first time a teacher undertook an interview activity with two year 3 boys, one of whom had speech language difficulties, she began by looking at a range of photos 'all about things that go on in school' spread over the desk. The activity at this point became one of identifying what could be seen as they became engrossed in the detail in the photos, descriptions that later spontaneously (and rather out of the blue) popped up in conversations subverting the discussion. On the one hand the photos provided a good ice breaker introducing a joint activity that facilitated interaction (Porter and Lacey 2005) but on the other-hand it gave the boys a false sense of what the 'activity' was about.

During the course of our observations a number of children in different settings stated that they didn't like assemblies or 'mat' time and when asked why, said they were just about talking. Activities therefore provided interest to what might otherwise be seen as a dull task. They also provided important time for reflection in a way that straight questions and answers do not (Punch 2002). The two specific activities that were adopted in this research used photographs and drawings.

Drawings had the advantage over photographs of focusing attention on thinking about a particular event of the child's choosing. This is useful for children with learning difficulties who can find it easier to talk about difficulties in the context of specific events rather than in a general sense (Connors and Stalker 2002). Where children had the skills to do so, drawing provided a time for re-constructing this event.

> Rhona: talking about her picture: 'I was only little I was about 5 with very very long hair then ... they did it on purpose ... angry ... didn't see them they ran and pushed me I was up in the air. Playtime ... big bandage.'

This then creates the conditions for discussion of the difficulties encountered and what made things more difficult and what helped. Carrying out the Point to Point activity, children having 'made their mark' to indicate their best and worst day, are then encouraged to draw a line between the two and consider where they are today and what would help them to move closer to their better day. Few children completed this activity, as staff introduced other aspects to the activity, including sorting photos along the line. Arguably, because of the quicker and often easy response required, this does not provide such a good vehicle for discussion as the slower pace of drawing.

For children with more limited language teachers chose to use talking mats. Originally this method was developed as a forum for involving young people with significant disabilities in important decision-making about their lives, but it has been adapted and used across a range of teaching and learning situations (Cameron and Murphy 2002; 2006; Germain 2005). Observations revealed that schools were using the idea in a variety of ways, not always placing three symbols to denote 'like' 'dislike' and 'so-so' on a board and inviting the child to place a symbol or photograph in a kind of sorting activity. Instead many staff developed the activity as revealed in the following observation in a primary school with pupils in Year R:

> Mrs Crosby working in a primary school with children with communication difficulties started by putting out pictures of food and asked children whether they wanted to put a smiley face on the picture or a sad face. When she felt they understood the activity she introduced pictures of different lessons and repeated the task. Then she introduced pictures of places and finally pictures of people.
> **Talking Mats Activity in a Reception Class**

This description reveals that the activity has been carefully structured to check that pupils understand the task. The introduction with food performs the same function as an icebreaker but without misleading children about the nature of the activity. She then introduces pictures of different lessons followed by aspects of the learning situation that extend the way children respond and parallels the type of questions used in the SEBD school. She has also made it a simpler activity than the original guidance by asking children to allocate one symbol to each picture in turn rather than expecting the pupils to sort them. The absence of a 'so-so' response however forces children to give a definite opinion, rather than allowing them a kind of 'neither like or dislike' or 'don't know' response, a situation that could lead to inaccuracies highlighting the importance of validating the responses. It provided the equivalent of a series of closed questions using concrete materials that reduce the demand on memory. For some children it may be necessary to devise a more individualised approach using photos specific to the pupil that illustrate them actually taking part in different lessons. This requires a greater level of planning and preparation.

Groupings

Schools adapted activities that had been devised as individual activities and carried them out as a group endeavour. This had many strengths and is consistent with a focus on making organisational changes to provide a more inclusive learning environment rather than focusing on individual needs. Groups help children to prod one another's memory, they give confidence and support from friends and can be more fun (Punch 2002). They also grant the relative safety for the novice teacher-researcher of making it more likely that some views will be proffered and avoid the downward spiral of discussion descending into question and answer with 'the questions getting longer and the answers shorter' (Ravet 2007). There is evidence to suggest that mainstream children may prefer group settings especially when talking generally about problems (Punch 2002). Schools used a range of group sizes including up to twelve children, although a more commonly recommended size for focus groups is 6–8 (Kruger and Casey 2000). There is also some suggestion that it can be better for girls (although not boys) to be in a single sex group (Curtis et al. 2004; Porter et al. 2008).

Group interviews may not be an appropriate context for those with more significant communication difficulties where the more articulate dominate discussion (Woolfson et al. 2007). The group format may also be challenging for those who find it difficult to take turns or who can get angry or impatient with their peers (Curtis et al. 2004) and for those who require a more individualised approach to communication (Woolfson et al. 2007). An individual setting can provide space to talk about more private or potentially embarrassing things and without the possibility of being interrupted (Punch 2002).

Conclusions

The challenge of ensuring that we consult with *all* children has been explored. This includes those with a disability and children who may be less articulate, including those who use augmentative and non-conventional systems of communication. While much of the literature supports the use of open questions, including open prompts, this is not necessarily a workable strategy with young children or with those with more limited communication skills. Here staff adopted a number of strategies using a 'supportive cradle' to promote responses. These involve providing a concrete context, personalizing the questions, checking on understanding by asking a similar question, leading through the questions to achieve a shared focus on the topic and asking yes/no questions. These strategies all have the potential to bias pupils' responses and it is important that we recognize and monitor this, validating the views expressed through additional measures.

Collecting the views of children on this important topic needs to be seen as an extended conversation rather than a checklist activity. Curtis et al. (2004) write about a cautious and unrushed approach to research with children with a disability.

It was notable through the observations that, while some children and teachers had greater experience of these types of conversations, for others this was the first time. In some schools there was a clear ethos of valuing children's strengths and recognizing that we all experience difficulties. Some settings therefore provided a more secure environment in which to disclose information.

Children need explanations of the relevance and importance of giving their "honest" views and if staff are confident to share details about aspects they find difficult they help to create a positive ethos towards difficulties and disabilities. In doing so it must be recognized that there is a difference between single event experiences and those which are more frequent and on-going. Some children said they disliked lessons that were just about talking so activities provide some relief from discussion but at the same time have the potential to promote a deeper reflection. The best included an icebreaker that was relevant to the aims of the activities and provided a space for joint interaction. Group discussion had a number of advantages but was not appropriate for all children and could be followed by opportunities for paired work or individual discussion.

The development work in schools emphasized the readiness of teachers to engage in discussions with children about schooling. This contribution has set out to confront some of the challenges of doing this and to encourage reflection on the ways in which different methods can constrain the data we collect. Responding creatively we can hone our approaches and ensure that the help given is both appropriate and sufficient for *all* pupils and that no one is missed out.

References

Antaki, C., N. Young, and M. Finlay. 2002. Shaping clients' answers: Departures from neutrality in care-staff interviews with people with a learning disability. *Disability & Society* 17, no. 4: 435–55.

Booth, T., and W. Booth. 1996. Sounds of silence: Narrative research with inarticulate subjects. *Disability & Society* 11, no. 1: 55–69.

Bruck, M., S. Ceci, and H. Hembrooke. 2002. The nature of children's true and false narratives. *Developmental Review* 22, no. 3: 520–54.

Cameron, L., and J. Murphy. 2002. Enabling young people with a learning disability to make choices at a time of transition. *British Journal of Learning Disabilities* 30: 105–12.

Cameron, L., and J. Murphy. 2006. Obtaining consent to participate in research: The issues involved in including people with a range of learning and communication disabilities. *British Journal of Learning Disabilities* 35: 113–20.

Cederburg, A-C., Y. Orbach, K. Sterberg, and M. Lamb. 2000. Investigative interviews of child witnesses in Sweden. *Child Abuse and Neglect* 24, no. 10: 1355–61.

Connors, C., and K. Stalker. 2002. *Children's experiences of disability: A positive outlook.* Interchange 75. Edinburgh: Scottish Executive.

Curtis, K., H. Roberts, J. Copperman, A. Downie, and K. Liabo. 2004. How come I don't get asked no questions? Researching 'hard to reach' children and teenagers. *Children and Family Social Work* 9: 167–75.

Deed, C. 2008. Disengaged boys' perspectives about learning. *Education 3–13* 36, no. 1: 3–14.

Department for Education and Skill/Disability Rights Commission. 2006. *Implementing the Disability Discrimination Act in schools and early years settings.* Nottingham: DfES.

Dockrell, J. 2004. How can studies of memory and language enhance the reliability of interviews? *British Journal of Learning Disabilities* 32, no. 4: 161–65.

Finlay, W.M.L., and E. Lyons. 2002. Acquiescence in interviews with people who have mental retardation. *Mental Retardation* 40, no. 1: 14–29.

Fritzley, V.H., and K. Lee. 2003. Do young children always say yes to yes–no questions? A metadevelopmental study of the affirmation bias. *Child Development* 74, no. 5: 1297–313.

Germain, R. 2005. *Type of educational provision made to young people with learning disabilities and participation in communities and activities beyond school.* PhD Thesis submitted to the University of Birmingham.

Hughes, M., and R. Grieve. 1980. On asking children bizarre questions. *First Language* 1, no. 2: 149–60.

Krahenbuhl, S., and M. Blades. 2006. The effect of question repetition within interviews on young children's eyewitness recall. *Journal of Experimental Child Psychology* 94: 57–67.

Krueger, R.A., and M.A. Casey. 2000. *Focus groups: A practical guide for applied research.* 3rd ed. London: Sage.

Lamb, M.E., and A. Fauchier. 2001. The effects of question type on self-contradictions by children in the course of forensic interviews. *Applied Cognitive Psychology* 15: 483–91.

Lambert, M. 2008. Devil in the detail: Using a pupil questionnaire survey in an evaluation of out-of-school classes for gifted and talented children. *Education 3–13* 36, no. 1: 69–78.

Lewis, A., and J. Porter. 2007. Research and pupil voice. In *Handbook of special education*, ed. L. Florian. London: Sage.

Mooney, A., C. Owen, and J. Statham. 2008. *Disabled children: Numbers, characteristics and local service provision.* Nottingham: DCSF.

Orbach, Y., and M.E. Lamb. 2001. The relationship between within-interview contradictions and eliciting interviewer utterances. *Child Abuse and Neglect* 25, no. 3: 323–33.

Porter, J., H. Daniels, J. Georgeson, A. Feiler, J. Hacker, B. Tarleton, V. Gallop, and D. Watson. 2008. *Disability data collection for children's services.* Research Report submitted DCFS-RR062. Nottingham: DCSF.

Porter, J., and P. Lacey. 2005. *Researching learning difficulties.* London: Sage.

Punch, S. 2002. Interviewing strategies with young people: The 'secret box'. Stimulus material and task-based activities. *Children & Society* 16: 45–56.

Ravet, J. 2007. Enabling pupil participation in a study of perceptions of disengagement: Methodological matters. *British Journal of Special Education* 34, no. 4: 234–42.

Stafford, A., A. Laybourn, and M. Hill. 2003. 'Having a say': Children and young people talk about consultation. *Children and Society* 17: 361–73.

Woolfson, R.C., M. Harker, D. Lowe, M. Shields, and H. Mackintosh. 2007. Consulting with Children and young people who have disabilities: Views of accessibility to education. *British Journal of Special Education* 34, no. 1: 40–9.

Wright, K. 2008. Researching the views of pupils with multiple and complex needs: Is it worth doing and whose interests are served by it? *Support for Learning* 23, no. 1: 32–40.

About face: visual research involving children

Caroline Lodge

Institute of Education, University of London, UK

Some crucial issues in visual research involving children in schools are examined: the contradictions between the current widespread practice of visual recordings in public and private spheres and the cautious approach adopted in educational research; the dominance of adults and text in school research despite technology providing accessible ways of using visual elements and involving young people; and the use of digital photography, which also poses questions about permissions and publication. All research involving young people raises issues about access, informed consent and power relations. Drawing on examples from my own research, it is argued that it is possible to adopt a critical stance in visual research rather than continue to reflect unequal power relations.

Introduction

This contribution explores some issues in visual research in schools, that is research that draws on data from visual images – such as drawings, diagrams, photographs and video recordings – to explore educational experiences. It draws attention to the dominance of text in research about schools and young people's educational experiences. Despite technology having provided some very accessible ways to involve visual elements in research and to enable young people to participate in the creation and production of data, this potential is rarely realised. Attention is also drawn to the exclusion by adults of young people's perspectives and participation in much educational research. Assumptions about identity and face need to be clarified, explored and challenged. Without a critical stance, research in schools and visual research itself will continue to reflect, reinforce and exacerbate existing unequal power relations within schools.

Here I am referring to assumptions and contradictions in the current use of digital images of people and especially of young people and of faces. The current widespread practice of visual recordings in public and private spheres, contrasts strongly with a cautious approach in research. This contrast was vividly illustrated at an educational conference in Auckland, New Zealand, in January 2008. Children from the local primary school, dressed in traditional costumes, performed Maori and Pacific Island dances at the start of each day of the conference. They were an attractive sight, and many delegates responded by taking photographs. Few of the educationalists present appeared to pause and consider the issues of the abuse of images, identification, informed consent, identity, ownership, publication and so on. This scene brought to my attention the tension between what is publicly acceptable and a cautious ethical stance in educational research. There are different rules for photography in different contexts: no restrictions apply for public performance but we are required to be very cautious in educational research. How does the tension play out? What different beliefs and values underlie it? What are the challenges thrown up by this tension?

I shall consider these issues by drawing on examples from my own research that involved visual contributions by children. This research developed from an earlier study of how an understanding of learning is limited or extended by participation in spoken discourse (Lodge 2001). The first of the two projects was an exploration of how the drawings of a Year (Y) 2 class in a primary school in an outer London borough can be read to consider their understandings of learning (Lodge 2007). The second project explored what happened when a Y4 class in a primary school in Kent, UK, were involved in the research project that involved identifying and taking digital photographs of things they found significant in their learning (called *What's important in my learning?*).

Experience from these projects suggests that while some research issues are not new, others have been created as a result of the technology that researchers might want to exploit: digital and web-based possibilities. Some ways forward will also be considered, in particular opening up the discussion so that research methods can take advantage of the technologies available.

Contradictions between public use and research of visual images involving children

In the public domain the use of visual imagery and of children's images in particular are widespread in:

- commercial use (eg: advertising using the appeal of children's images);
- promotional material by schools (eg: children's images used to decorate text in order to create a desired image of a school);
- newspapers and newscasts eg: young people are seen as both a danger and as in danger (Prout and Hallett 2003) alongside celebration of their achievements;
- security and surveillance (eg: there were 4.2 million CCTV cameras in 2006, the contradictions inherent in their use are tellingly exposed in an episode in *The Accidental*, when a young girl uses a camcorder to film CCTV cameras to the consternation of a security guard (Ali 2005);
- finding children (eg: lost and found children's images on websites following the tsunami of 2004, and Madeleine McCann from 2007);
- personal use (eg: at family events, children's performances, tourist sites and so forth); and
- easy circulation via the Internet and other means (eg: Youtube and jpegs of digital photographs).

There is a contradiction between this largely indiscriminate use, and limited and fearful use in educational research.

Identification of individuals by others is a concern in schools. In my own research in UK schools concerns about identification of individual children and manipulation of their images have frequently been raised by headteachers and teachers. I have been asked to alter names that appeared on posters within drawings of classrooms. Teachers are concerned that children may be identified if their images appear on the Internet, and this can be used to approach or groom them. They also fear that paedophiles, or parents, excluded from access by the courts, may locate children in this way. Often schools use first names only when labelling photographs on their websites to reduce this risk. The response in schools is usually taken to avoid litigation. It is very common for schools to have asked parents, on the admission of their child, to sign a consent or release form, often with differential agreements about usage (in printed or online material, where their face can be recognised or only the back of the head seen, and so forth).

In the public domain such caution was abandoned in the summer of 2007 when Madeleine McCann went missing in Portugal. Most people in Europe (and further afield) saw her face many times over, in newspapers, on the TV, sent via email with a request to send it on to everyone in their address book. Online news pages and other sites created electronic links to the website set up by her parents (from which images of Madeleine could be downloaded). Leaving no stone unturned, as the slogan on the *findmadeleine* website had it, means that ways of identifying and finding people now frequently include electronic or virtual means. Many people suggested that the use of the Internet in this search made it more likely that Madeleine will be (or has been) killed or have to undergo plastic surgery and that her image is more likely to have been used by paedophiles.

A second concern expressed in schools is that of manipulation by paedophiles. There is a widespread view that manipulation of an image somehow violates the person pictured: at least in photography (it doesn't happen with drawings as far as I am aware). The assumption or belief is that if the image of you is manipulated, you are being manipulated. This is close to the apocryphal idea in aboriginal or primitive beliefs that to be photographed is to give up a piece of oneself or of one's soul. It is probably the case that people have different beliefs about how far identity is bound up with, even captured by, the photographed image. In educational research caution is trumping creativity.

Adults in schools are rarely concerned about a different kind of manipulation – the use of images of children to decorate school publicity in a way that uses the intrinsic appeal of vulnerability. Hart (1997) cautions that non-participative forms of involving young people are tokenistic, decorative, or even exploitative. Researchers could also be tempted to decorate their research with images of children, which would be both exploitative and manipulative.

The technology available develops rapidly and so people have had to learn to use it in research and to become visually literate (Kress and van Leeuwen 1996). The possibilities of using digital images are largely unexplored in research. As I have suggested, schools impose a conservative approach, influenced by public panics about the sexual exploitation of their images which identify children. As a result schools and researchers are reproducing existing power relations, so that adults continue to take responsibility for all the research processes and exclude the young people from participation.

This is being challenged by such initiatives as *Students as researchers* and by recent explorations into some innovative practices (Fielding and Bragg 2003; Thomson 2008a, 2008b). These innovative practices start from the beliefs that young people have the capacity to express themselves and the right to do so, and that expressing themselves can include visual means (Thomson 2008a). These are exceptions in a field dominated by adults' agendas and by text-based research.

Use of visual images in research

That which is acceptable in the everyday photography of people and children is at odds with the practices of research. Researchers must consider the ethics of using digital photographic methods, just as they must with any research design. The current dominant approach is largely cautious and involves the application of ethical considerations based on word-based research, rather an explicit engagement within the research community of the specific issues.

I was provoked into thinking about photographing faces in educational research by a session at an earlier educational research conference, in 2007, in Canada. Jenna Kelland, from the University of Alberta, described her research into adult women's online learning. She began with photographs by the participants to represent aspects of their learning. The photographs were then annotated by the person who took them and the photographs and commentary used to stimulate online dialogue between the participants. I was interested in this innovative research because Jenna was:

- looking at a new format for learning (online);
- looking at a relatively under-researched group (women in higher education);
- bringing a co-constructivist approach to learning and to the research; and
- using innovative methods of inquiry (photography, online interactions).

Jenna was concerned about possible vulnerabilities of the research participants. She initially thought she would not use digital photography and she would exclude photographs of people, reflecting a concern that digital photography can easily be manipulated to distort images. Her concerns were related to issues of anonymity, privacy and confidentiality. Excluding people appeared to be the equivalent of giving research subjects anonymity and pseudonyms.

On this occasion the two issues of privacy and distortion were resolved through the option of disposable cameras, and the signing of release forms giving permission both for the use of the images in the online discussions and by Jenna. She is now both engaged in researching the possibilities of new technologies in education (online learning) but also using the potential of new technology as a tool for research. She provides an example of some resolutions to some of the problematics of using the technologies as a research tool.

For the researcher, the main concern is not to avoid litigation, although to retain the goodwill of the school the honouring of the permissions is important, but to gain the informed consent of the young participants. In my projects the school staff did not consider it necessary to go further than parental permission and ask permission of the children on their own behalf. The schools' consent agreements assume that the parents or carers are entitled to give permission on behalf of the young people, and no further consent is required. In my experience it is judicious to have such consent from the adults, but in no way are such generalised permissions sufficient to satisfy educational research ethical standards of informed consent. Guidelines such as those of the British Education Research Association (see www.bera.ac.uk) that emphasise proper respect and avoiding harm are useful here. Further, researchers should not add to the large amount of direction given by adults to young people in schools.

Consent by the young people presents challenges. Alderson and Morrow (2004) suggest that an ethical approach to consent implies proper information and freely given consent. Such an approach includes ensuring that there is no potential or actual harm to the participants, as well as understanding that harm might be defined differently by researchers and participants.

In the *Regarding learning* project I asked the pupils to take photographs within their classroom. These were to be used later in a large format book about their learning in their classroom. I gained unanimous parental permission for their children to participate. I also asked the children for their permissions for me to take photographs of them in their classroom. One child wanted to be excluded from my photographs. I asked if he would compromise by being given the power to exclude the use of any photographs in which he appeared, but he did not want me to take any photographs of him. Excluding him presented me with physical challenges as I was keen to be as inclusive as possible and to involve his table partner. I did not fully understand the boy's objections, but I did honour his request. In some cases, young people's choices could prevent the photography from proceeding.

Sometimes providing information about the research and the participation that is requested by the young people can feel very long-winded. However, it is important to check that one is not misleading them. 'Are we going to be famous?' asked a Y4 child when I was explaining about publishing what I wrote up. I tried to explain the difference between photo-journalism in *Hello!* and a paper in an academic journal. The children were disappointed by the kind of publicity that my answer implied.

In research using drawings and photographs I have been faced with the question of who has ownership of the artefacts and the power to reproduce them. Ownership of an image might be invested in a number of people. One photograph in the *Regarding learning* project was the idea of one child, taking the picture was directed by another, a third actually pressed the button, the class used the picture for a class book and two people posed for it. In addition, I supplied the camera, film and print and also have a digital version, which gives me technological power to reproduce the image. To whom does the photograph belong and who should decide how it can be used and who can use it, to say what and about whom and to whom? Who is the researcher? Who can control the use of such research data? Ownership, control, interpretation are all contestable and distributed. Louise Alcoff describes such contradictory views:

> On one view, the author of a text [or in this case a photograph] is its 'owner and originator' credited with creating its ideas and with being their authoritative interpreter. On another view, the original speaker or writer [or photographer] is no more privileged than any other person who articulates these views, and in fact the 'author' cannot be identified in a strict sense because the concept of author is an ideological construction many abstractions removed from the way in which ideas emerge and become material forces. (Alcoff 1991)

The difficulties recognised by Alcoff (1991) in her exploration of the problem of speaking for others are those that had to be addressed in these research projects. The difficulties were made more complex because the 'text' being read and its meaning being made were images rather than words, as the example of the photograph just described shows. Relational issues are embedded in Alcoff's problem and abound in the conjunction of visual research and the participation of young people. For example, researchers might find it hard to decide on who is the subject of a research project where the young people are both creating the data and its objects. Who should decide what meanings are given to the photograph and how? How can research located in, and mediated through, the school do other than reproduce existing power relationships, or invite the young people to collude in them? Unless the young people themselves are active in the research processes – for example helping to create and to derive meaning from images – then the tendency for adults to create their own answers will endure.

The value of visual research in education

Given all the difficulties and tensions outlined above, why might anyone want to use digital image research in schools? I want to offer three main reasons. First, digital technology opens up some interesting possibilities for researchers, albeit in a context dominated by text. Text is generally privileged in educational research, text as material for analysis and as the mode of communicating findings (Prosser 1998). Second, digital image research offers a very accessible way for young people to become active in the research process themselves, to reverse the normal role of having research done to them, and allow them to participate more in this process (Thomson 2008a). The third reason is pedagogic and is about the value of young people learning about images.

a. The possibilities of digital research for researchers

My first claim is that digital technology opens up some interesting possibilities for researchers. Young people can know and express knowledge not available to others, and it is worth eliciting this knowledge. However, researchers may need an alternative to more the conventional methods of interviewing and surveys. As Burnard noted, methods that rely on the spoken or written words (interviews or questionnaires and surveys) do not reveal all that is known by a young person:

> Children know more than they know they know. They surely know more about what they know than the researcher does. Most of what they know, they know implicitly. Knowledge is not filed away in pupils' heads in answer form waiting for the stimulus of the perfect question to release it. No researcher has ever found out what it means to be a new age traveller's child or a foster child or a teenage mother by asking directly, 'What does it mean to be a …?' The purpose of image-based techniques in interviews is to get them to represent what they know, feel and think about what they know – and to help them to talk. (Burnard 2002)

b. The possibilities of digital research for the participation of young people

My second and connected claim is that the creation of images (drawings, video or photography) can offer opportunities for the usually silenced and marginalised to participate, and perhaps to alter prevailing power relationships. Kaplan and Howes (2004) describe the creation of a contact zone (a website) where differently empowered people – teachers and students – could interact. As their project's title suggests *Seeing through different eyes* invites participants to consider alternative views and meanings through dialogue about images produced by young people.

Sometimes using digital images produced by young people will challenge accepted wisdom and assumptions underpinning practice in schools. Research using images produced by young people has the potential, in Foucauldian terms, to make the familiar strange through familiar scenes being seen from another's point of view (see, for example, Lodge 2007). Images also capture the messiness of the world, of learning, of human relationships, the nuances and complexities that are denied in the policy world.

One example is Stacey's drawing from the *Regarding learning* project (Figure 1).

Stacey (who was about 6 years old) drew her picture with mixed perspectives, showing the view from her seat, including the teacher who has yellow hair, as well as something like a view from above. She has shown five children sitting at separate desks, each with a border separating them from each other and a mysterious number in one corner (0, 12, 2, 1 and 10). Everyone has a big smile. The children have workbooks open on their desks. There are sums on the whiteboard. The full drawing of each child is visible through the brown coloured desk. A key feature of Stacey's drawing is the separation of the children from each other through the arrangement of the desks. In her image of learning the pupils sit separately facing the teacher. In Stacey's classroom there was no space between adjacent tables. It was very crowded, and the tables were arranged in two horseshoes. Despite the crowded and busy appearance of the classroom in my photographs, Stacey's drawing represents the experience of learning as separated from her classmates.

In many research projects young people remain passive, providing information, rather than being engaged in designing the research, analysing the data, or disseminating the findings. Going further than simply providing the data often means using mixed methods approaches, as research including images often does (Morrow 1999), where the images are intended to supplement other material. The Mosaic approach (Clark 2005), as its name suggests, is a mixed methods framework

Figure 1.   Stacey's drawing of learning in the classroom (reproduced with permission).

for listening to young children specifically about their learning environment. Schratz and Steiner-Loffler (1998) have also used pupil photographs to contribute to school self-evaluation.

c. The value for young people of learning about images

My third claim refers to the pedagogic value of image research. The participation of young people in creating images for research is required for them to understand the world in which they are growing up. Unlike writing, photography (like drawing) is not a valued or a privileged activity in the school curriculum and therefore young people do not receive much guidance. Digital photography is often on display, especially in primary classrooms in the UK, but most often as a record or a decoration, not as a sense-making tool. Visual literacy, the ability to read images and to understand their use, and to be critical of visual elements of the environment, is increasingly necessary, especially among the young (Kress and van Leeuwen 1996).

Images used in research require the participation of young people to provide contextual information in order to make meaning. This means that when we undertake research we have to listen to young people and what they tell us about the images and their creation. In this way the young people become the subject rather than the object in the research, and in some cases participants in the research. Why is this so? It is often said that 'photographs don't lie', and that 'the picture speaks for itself'. This is seldom the case. Images are rarely able to make a statement without textual explanation. We usually need to know the context of an image in order to understand it (Becker 1995). We need captions, details of the time, place of its creation and something about the artist (documenter, journalist, artist, tourist etc).

An example of the importance of captions was in the classroom display that was an outcome of a project with Y4 children called *What's important in our learning?* Each picture had a caption to explain the significance of the photograph and the reason for the inclusion of the object or activity in the display. The caption had the additional purpose of getting the children to articulate in words something about their learning and the relationship of the object or process to their learning. Their photographs included other people, equipment, attitudes (such as listening or concentration). The additional verbal or textual information helped us to read, that is to understand, the images and also helped the teacher and the young people to understand more about their perceptions of what helped their learning.

One of the most emancipatory aspects of using images in research is that to understand or read the images we need the participation of the young people who produced them. This may be by inviting young people to talk about their photographs. Alternatively, the researcher may rely on other research methods. For example, the Y2 class that produced drawings of learning in the classroom was later provided with disposable cameras and invited to take pictures to do with learning over several weeks. According to their class teacher, decisions to take a photograph provoked frequent discussions about the photographers' intentions (such as 'What's that got to do with learning?' 'Can we take a photograph in Assembly?' 'What's that a picture of?') The discussions about learning and what the children noticed about learning led to very rich conversations in that classroom.

Not all of the concerns about who participates, who is included, selected and so forth are particular to visual research. This does not mean that they do not need to be attended to. The issues of power in the research relationship cannot be avoided.

The adult researcher may be viewed as just another teacher, as I found in a primary school classroom when a child appealed to me to sort out a wrangle between him and his friend. However, increased familiarity also led to more informality in the photographs they took of me and of each other with my camera. On that occasion being seen as equivalent to another teacher enhanced the opportunities for dialogue. This is not always the case as suggested by the title of Morrow's article 'If you were a teacher, it would be harder to talk to you' (Morrow 1999).

This is not an argument against ethical considerations of respect, trust and preventing harm. Young people deserve at least as much of these as any other research participants (Alderson and Morrow 2004). Indeed I am arguing for a more active participation by young people in educational research in schools. It is an argument against reaction that assumes that anonymity is always desirable, and that smudging or pixilation of images is the visual equivalent of anonymising text. Anonymity can act to silence as well as to protect. It is an argument for gaining consent not as a means to protect the adults (Heath et al. 2007), but rather not only as an opportunity to engage young people in dialogue about their interests but also to go further and participate in clarifying the purposes and design of the research, the production and analysis of data, and the dissemination of the findings.

Conclusion

I have suggested that research in schools is dominated by both adults and text and that the use of images of, and created by, young people opens up many possibilities for researchers, and for the participation of more young people in research processes. I have indicated that the cautious response adopted by the research community to such research is in contrast to the rapidly proliferating visual context in which we live our lives, and in which images are being indiscriminately obtained. I have drawn on examples of engagement in visual research that provided opportunities for young people to develop a more critical understanding of their learning environment. In short, this contribution is an argument for more open debate among educational researchers, more inclusion of young people in research activities, and for the more widespread use of visual material to do this.

References

Alcoff, L.M. 1991. The problem of speaking for others. *Cultural Critique* 20: 5–32.
Alderson, P., and V. Morrow. 2004. *Ethics, social research and consulting with children and young people*. Ilford: Barnardo's.
Ali, M. 2005. *The accidental*. London: Penguin.
Becker, H.S. 1995. Visual sociology, documentary photography, and photojournalism: It's (almost) all a matter of context. *Visual Sociology* 10, nos. 1–2: 5–14.
Burnard, P. 2002. Using image-based techniques in researching pupil perspectives. *Communicating* 5: 2–3.
Clark, A. 2005. Ways of seeing: Using the mosaic approach to listen to young children's perspectives. In *Beyond listening: Children's perspectives on early childhood services*, ed. A. Clark, A.T. Kjorholt, and P. Moss. Bristol: Policy Press.
Fielding, M., and S. Bragg. 2003. *Students as researchers: Making a difference*. Cambridge: Pearson Publishing.
Hart, R. 1997. *Children's participation: The theory and practice of involving young citizens in community development and environmental care*. London: Earthscan Publications Ltd with UNICEF.

Heath, S., V. Charles, G. Crow, and R. Wiles. 2007. Informed consent, gatekeepers and go-betweens: Negotiating consent in child- and youth-orientated institutions. *British Educational Research Journal* 33, no. 3: 403–17.

Kaplan, I., and A. Howes. 2004. 'Seeing through different eyes': Exploring the value of participative research using images in schools. *Cambridge Journal of Education* 34, no. 2: 143–55.

Kress, G., and T. van Leeuwen. 1996. *Reading images: The grammar of visual design*. London: Routledge.

Lodge, C. 2001. *An investigation into discourses of learning in schools*. Unpublished EdD, University of London, Institute of Education, London.

Lodge, C. 2007. Regarding learning: Children's drawings of learning in the classroom. *Learning Environments Research* 10: 145–56.

Morrow, V. 1999. If you were a teacher, it would be harder to talk to you: Reflections on qualitative research with children in school. *International Journal of Social Research Methodology* 1, no. 4: 297–313.

Prosser, J. 1998. The status of image-based research. In *Image-based research: A sourcebook for qualitative researchers*, ed. J. Prosser, 97–112. London: Routledge Falmer.

Prout, A., and C. Hallett. 2003. Introduction. In *Hearing the voices of children: Social policy for a new century*, ed. C. Hallett and A. Prout. London: Routledge Falmer.

Schratz, M., and U. Steiner-Loffler. 1998. Pupils using photographs in school self-evaluation. In *Image-based research: A sourcebook for qualitative researchers*, ed. J. Prosser. London: Routledge Falmer.

Thomson, P. 2008a. Children and young people: Voices in visual research. In *Doing visual research with children and young people*, ed. P. Thomson, London: Routledge.

Thomson, P. ed. 2008b. *Doing visual research with children and young people*. London: Routledge.

Children researching their urban environment: developing a methodology

Elisabeth Barratt Hacking[a] and Robert Barratt[b]

[a]Department of Education, University of Bath, UK; [b]School of Education, Bath Spa University, UK

Listening to children: environmental perspectives and the school curriculum (L2C) was a UK research council project based in schools in a socially and economically deprived urban area in England. It focused on 10/12 year old children's experience of their local community and environment, and how they made sense of this in relation both to their lives and the school curriculum. Issues faced by the research team in developing and implementing the project methods are explored including the challenge to promote children's equal involvement with adults in all aspects of the research. A case is made for promoting participatory and collaborative research with children in school settings. It is suggested that through the L2C project, the children developed an approach that was sensitive to children's personal experience and that developed their capacity as researchers and their understanding of the value of research.

Introduction

Research that makes the most of children's abilities, and treats them with respect, can provide children with opportunities that bring significant improvements in their own wellbeing. These include greater opportunities to acquire knowledge, to develop new skills, to build new friendships and wider support networks, to be heard and to have their concerns taken seriously. (Save The Children 2004, 10)

This contribution discusses some of the methodological challenges faced when undertaking participatory research with children aged 10–12 years. It draws on the experience of research in schools in England (Staffordshire and South Gloucestershire) which focused on children's local urban environment experience. A pilot research project was conducted in a school in Staffordshire (Barratt and Barratt Hacking 2008). This was the genesis of '*Listening to children (L2C): environmental perspectives and the school curriculum*', a project undertaken by University of Bath researchers with children and teachers from a secondary school and one of its feeder primary schools in South Gloucestershire (see e.g. Barratt Hacking et al. 2007; Barratt Hacking, Scott, and Barratt 2007). In both projects the schools involved recognised the potential of listening to children's local experiences and involving children in local environment research in order to take account of children's concerns and so contribute to their wellbeing.

The L2C project is used to exemplify methodological challenges in research with children. A range of issues are explored that the Research Team faced in developing and implementing the methodology and methods for the project. Primarily, the project aimed to develop context-specific research approaches designed by children that would gain access to 10–12 year old children's personal experience of the urban environment. In this contribution the background to the L2C research project is provided. The rationale for local environment research with children and the methodological challenges of participatory research are explained. The methodological approach is illustrated using examples of children's research from the L2C Project. Finally, reflections on the experience of researching with children are used to provide insights for researching with 10–12 year old children.

Background to the Listening to Children Project

Listening to children: environmental perspectives and the school curriculum (L2C) was a UK research council project (RES-221-25-0036, ESRC Environment and Human Behaviour Programme) based in schools in a socially and economically deprived urban area in South Gloucestershire. The project set out to investigate how children's local environmental perspectives might become a part of their school curriculum experience. The research was undertaken by a Research Team comprising of sixteen 11/12 year old children and four of their 16/17 year old mentors, two teachers, a parent and four university researchers. It focused on 10/12 year old children's experience of their local community and environment, and how they make sense of this in relation both to their lives and the school curriculum. This area exemplifies the sorts of social, economic, environmental and educational challenges that urban communities are facing nationally, and in the developed world more generally, and there is concern about the impact of such environments on children's wellbeing (Sustainable Development Commission 2008). The school recognised the need to involve local people in school development, and the L2C project provided an opportunity to involve parents, children and local voluntary bodies in curriculum change.

The L2C project aimed to explore:

(1) 10–12 year old children's experience in the local environment and community.
(2) How the curriculum can become more relevant to children, their families and the local community, and ways of involving children in both curriculum development and action in the local community.
(3) How local environmental and educational policy can change to take account of children's perspectives.

These aims reflect national and international agendas to improve education and the environment at the local scale, for example, in the sustainable schools guidance for schools in England (Sustainable Schools n.d.) and in local sustainability initiatives proposed at the Earth Summit (Earth Summit 2002). L2C provided key opportunities to consider how the community and its schools, parents, children and teachers can meet the challenge of growing up in an urban setting. It also explored ways of making closer connections between children's everyday experience and the school curriculum whilst enhancing children's opportunity to make a positive contribution in the school and local context (DfES 2003). There is evidence to suggest that children still have limited opportunities to contribute to school and local development (see, for example, Ofsted 2007; Roe 2007).

The two phases of the study were:

Phase 1 which involved establishing and planning the project then gathering and analysing evidence about the nature of 10–12 year old pupils' local environment experience (May 2004–December 2004); and

Phase 2 which used the evidence gathered and analysed in Phase 1 to develop, implement and evaluate a curriculum project (January 2004–May 2005).

Here the first phase of the project is mainly drawn upon, in particular, the nature of 10–12 year-old pupils' local environment experience (Research aim 1) in order to illustrate a number of methodological challenges in undertaking participatory research with children.

Why do local environment research with children?

The research discussed adopted an ecological perspective; in this the child is viewed within their family, social, environmental and cultural context. It is widely acknowledged that child development is not just biological but is also a product of experience (Kagan 1994; UNICEF 2004). The authors' interest in environmental education and environmental learning in schools is underpinned by a belief that children's everyday experience of their local community and environment is a significant influence on their learning and development (Barratt and Barratt Hacking 2008; see also Baacke 1985; Bronfenbrenner 1979; van Matre 1979). Evidence from the pilot Staffordshire project suggested a dissonance between the child's local experience and the school curriculum and that the children welcomed the opportunity to share their community experience in school and consider its relevance to the school curriculum (Barratt and Barratt Hacking 2008).

The rationale for undertaking local environment research with children is also based on the premise that communities need to engage those in the present who will determine future needs and wants. The UN Convention on the Rights of the Child set a global agenda for children's participation in democratic societies (United Nations 1989). In England, the Children's Bill and the new Children's Commissioner require that local authorities recognise the contribution made by children to society (DfES 2003). There is a policy commitment that children will 'actively be involved in shaping all decisions that affect their lives' (Children's Commissioner n.d.). Engaging children in local research can provide children with the skills and opportunities to make a contribution to society through local decision making:

> Children's participation (in research) makes children more active citizens as it . . . challenges the status quo in terms of what children can realistically contribute and accomplish'. (Save the Children 2004, 14)

Local research can therefore support children in:

- making stronger links between their everyday experience and learning in school (and so enhancing the relevance of the school curriculum for children and communities);

- developing a deeper knowledge and understanding of the everyday local environment and its links with other environments;
- using children's research findings to formulate and pursue their aspirations for the local environment, for themselves, others and for wildlife; and
- developing capacity as researchers and as local citizens, for example, by applying research skills and findings to their current and future role as consumers, residents, employees, stakeholders and voters.

Developing genuine participation and participatory research in a school setting

Participatory research has been defined as an approach that:

> gives a 'voice' to those being researched, by questioning the acquisition and usefulness of knowledge, the power relationship between the researchers and the researched, and the stance of the 'objective' researcher. (Clark 2004)

This form of research developed out of concerns to i) understand the experience of community members and ii) work towards community improvement through providing opportunities for members to be partners in research. Examples include work with less advantaged communities and children (Hart 1997) and recipients of health services (Laws et al. 1999). The development of participation and participatory research has been less evident in school settings where 'providers and policy-makers have been slower to realise the potential of consulting "consumers"' (Flutter and Rudduck 2004, xi). However 'there is clear evidence that the political and social climate has begun to warm to the principle of involving children and young people but we must wait to see whether schools will provide the right conditions for pupil voice to grow' (Flutter and Rudduck 2004, 139).

Participation and participatory research is interpreted differently by different researchers and in different contexts. De Koning and Martin (1996, p. 3) suggest a range of interpretations including where the researcher and research community design the research together in contrast to where researchers design the study and then collect data with the help of the community. The approach adopted for the L2C project represents the former interpretation, also described as 'researching collaboratively with children' (Barratt and Barratt Hacking 2008; Garbarino, Stott, and Faculty of the Erikson Institute 1989). Children and young people are one of the most heavily researched groups in society. However, despite attempts to get beyond mere observation to extended dialogue with young people and reporting findings in their own words, the process still tends to be controlled by professional adults, that is, teachers and researchers (Clark et al. 2001; Kellet 2005a):

> There is a lot of research done by adults 'on', 'about', and even 'for' children, but very little research in which children play an active and meaningful role. (Researching children n.d.)

In contrast the intention was that children would take an equal responsibility in developing all stages of the research from agreeing research questions through to developing methods, analysis, evaluation and dissemination. However, the opportunity for children to be genuine participants in a school-based research project can be limited by issues of compliance. The L2C project began to tackle such issues by adopting a participatory and collaborative approach to the research. This approach reflects a trend in educational and social science research from research *on* children to research *with* children and, more recently, towards the 'new paradigm' of research *by* children which involves 'children as active researchers' (Kellet 2005a, 2005b; see also Alderson 2000, 2001; Christensen and Allison 2000; Kirby 2004b).

Responding to research design issues in collaborative research with children

Four issues in collaborative research with children are discussed in the following sections:

1.   Establishing genuine consent to participate

> Consent in research ... involves taking time to decide, being able to ask questions about the research, and then being able to say yes or no. Consent should be also seen as ongoing, rather than as a one-off event. (Morrow 2008, 54)

Within ethical debates surrounding research and children there is recognition of the difficulty of obtaintaining reliable consent in school settings. This relates to the notion that children will consent to adult expectations in relation to work and behaviour (Miller and Bell 2002; David 2007). In this respect 'assumed consent' (Heath et al. 2004), where the gatekeepers (teachers, senior managers) consent to participation on children's behalf, means that children do not necessarily exercise choice about their involvement. For example, children may believe that a research project is just part of normal class or school work and therefore that they are expected to participate in it (David, Edwards, and Aldred 2001; Morrow 1999). For these reasons there was a concern in the L2C project to ensure that children genuinely consented to participate and understood their right to withdraw as the project developed.

Prior to the involvement of children the school- and university-based researchers explored ways of approaching the issues around informed consent. The idea to open up the project to volunteers (through a year group assembly led by the teacher researchers followed by a question and answer session) attempted to ensure that:

(i) the project was presented in an appropriate way for 11/12 year olds;
(ii) children understood what they were volunteering for, the risks involved and expectations of them; and
(iii) there was equality of opportunity.

Out of about 200 children in the assembly, 50 stayed behind to ask questions and decide whether to volunteer. Through a negotiated process, eight girls and eight boys (representing all the tutor groups, a range of scholastic ability, parental background, in-school behaviour, and motivation to study) joined a parent, two teachers and university researchers in the Research Team.

In the first Research Team meeting ethical issues were explored including confidentiality and mutual expectations of the project. Children's right to withdraw from the project was discussed and clarified at the outset, repeated in writing to parents/ carers and revisited at different stages of the research. Children were offered debriefing if they decided to withdraw; one child chose to withdraw part way through the project and requested debriefing. These and similar matters were revisited throughout the life of the project. The emergent nature of L2C's research design meant that the project started out with research aims and questions but not with a fully determined research design. The approach that developed came out of a process of discussion and negotiation with children and hence consent to participate became an ongoing process as the project evolved.

2. *Developing appropriate and valid research methods and considering safety issues in the subsequent data gathering*

The L2C project adopted an *emergent* research design in that participants shaped the direction of the project through a process of discussion and negotiation. The Research Team met weekly in one hour off timetable sessions and began to focus on developing research methods. The challenge was to find ways of empowering children to use skills that are usually conducted in an adult domain associated with developing and implementing social science research methods. The approach adopted attempted to develop the children's skills and confidence as researchers whilst building on their natural research skills, for example, enquiring minds and ability to ask questions together with their interest and expertise in using technology. It also recognised children's ability to design:

appropriate and innovative research tools which help to engage young respondents in research. (Kirby 2004b, 276)

In an early Research Team meeting the children:

(i) explored their understandings of the term 'local environment and community';
(ii) planned how they might find out about how other children behave in the local environment; and
(iii) considered how they might research children's likes, dislikes and feelings about the locality.

In addition, there was a focus on developing research skills for data gathering such as designing questionnaires, interview techniques and using information and communication technology (ICT) equipment including dictaphones and digital cameras. This was an essential first step in building children's capacity to engage in research and thus participate fully in the project.

The children's ideas were used as the basis for all decision making, for example, some children suggested making video and photographic diaries of their local experience using mobile telephones. The children also suggested asking groups of children who lived near each other to compile a large 'neighbourhood' map reflecting their local experience. There were also opportunities for the children to seek advice from the adult researchers who largely acted as facilitators. Through a negotiated process, the child members of the Research Team decided that they would gather data, not only from their year group peers in school, but also from younger, primary aged children who would join the school the following year. The research instruments included:

- Children's photographic and video diaries of their local environment experience (using mobile phone technology and digital cameras).
- Children's personal maps (with a children's questionnaire) which the children termed the 'little map' for all the year group at secondary school (90 children) and 20 children from the primary school.

- Children's group map drawn on a very large sheet of paper by a group of children who live in the same neighbourhood which the children termed the 'big map' (primary school children).
- Group interview 1 discussing the group neighbourhood map (primary school children).
- Group interview 2: discussing children's individual personal maps and annotating a digital version of the local street map (primary school children).
- Parents'/carers' (and grandparents) group interview.
- Curriculum audit (for teachers).

The research instruments were developed by the children in consultation with the adult researchers across the following weeks. Some issues arose with the photographic and video diaries; the children wanted to make weekend diaries of how they used their independent time in the locality with digital cameras. However, through discussion the team decided that this was inadvisable as it would be impossible to safeguard children from becoming targets whilst using expensive equipment in the community. Equally, the team was concerned about the ethical issues related to capturing images of children. In a compromise the children kept diaries using their personal mobile telephones and avoided capturing images of children not working in the L2C project.

In terms of the questionnaires, maps and group interviews 10–11 year olds from a nearby feeder primary school were invited to the school for a day during which the Research Team children conducted a circus of research activities with support from the adult researchers. As the subjects were younger this provided an opportunity to develop confidence in interviewing. The group interview sessions demonstrated how effectively the children were able to illicit younger children's thinking about their environmental experience by using child-friendly language, appropriately phrased questions and putting them at ease (Kirby 2004a). The children built on this experience by sharing responsibility for joining tutor group sessions in their own school to set up and conduct the questionnaires for their whole year group.

The adult researchers had anticipated that the children would find it difficult to engage in the development of research methods. However, this did not materialise:

> What we actually delivered over time was generated by the pupils ... down to individual (questionnaire) questions ... the balance of child and adult decision making was probably 70:30 towards children ... we facilitated children's decision making. (teacher researcher)

3.   *Engaging children in the complexities of data analysis*

In the next stage of the project the Research Team faced the task of analysing a range of data sets that had been gathered from ninety 11–12 year olds in their school and around twenty 10–11 year olds from a feeder primary school. The Research Team held a two day Data Analysis Conference to begin this task; the children worked for most of the time in small groups supported by four year 12 mentors (16/17 year olds) who had volunteered to join the L2C project.[1] These older students were able to bring a range of expertise to the data analysis including their greater experience in the local community and their own research and ICT skills.

The data analysis was also facilitated by one of the university researchers who introduced a qualitative framework for the analysis of each data set as follows:

- You will need to read, look at maps, listen to the audio tape or look at the video in order to familiarise yourself with the data. Do this on an individual or group basis, whatever seems best.
- Re-look at the data, start to think about what is important about what children are saying.
- Make notes of what strikes you as important – each point should be added to a sticky 'post it' note.
- Talk to your partner add your notes to his/her notes.
- Make one set of notes for the whole group using the lap top.
- Organise your notes into different groups of ideas.

After initial support from the university and teacher researchers the groups worked mostly independently of adults and, as a consequence, this enabled the children to avoid adult interpretations:

> Participation of children in research can often produce better quality data, as it helps … clarify the analysis and the interpretation of data. New insights are provided by children. (Save the Children 2004, 13)

Part way through the two days each small group interviewed a sample of children from whom they had gathered the data to corroborate the findings. This corroboration process gave the children confidence that their findings were sound and valid.

The data analysis conference concluded with presentations of findings from each group to an audience made up of the Research Team including the university- and school-based researchers involved in the project, the Head teacher and the two Deputy Head teachers. This gave the team the opportunity to synthesise their findings and review interim findings about children's local environment and community experience (Figure 1). This also built children's confidence; for the first time their work was disseminated and an important and influential audience was listening to them. The children's reflections on the analysis phase demonstrated a heightened awareness about children's experience of the local environment and that they were starting to consider the relationship between their local community and school experience:

> I've learnt that not everyone thinks we're being taught enough that's relevant outside school and for us later on so it's great to give our views. (Shane, year 8)

The adult members of the Research Team were surprised by the way in which the children approached this new and complex task. Kirby suggests that analysis has to be taken on by adults or shared between adults and children as it is 'one of the hardest stages of participatory research' and perceived by children as, 'difficult' and 'boring' (2004b, 278). In contrast Bragg suggests that although 'young co-researchers tend not to get involved in data analysis … where they have been in control of the process, their involvement has been shown to be successful' (2007, 19). This latter point is reflected in the L2C project; the children responded positively to the challenge of analysing their data and, with the support of their mentors, worked mostly independently of adults.

1. **Children have an intricate knowledge of their local community and consider the quality of their local environment to be of great importance.**
   - *We have similar concerns and interests about the community and environment ... 'personal' (e.g. health, family and friends), 'safety / danger' (e.g. people, roads, vandalism), 'play' and 'shopping'.*
   - *Most of us move around without adults now... on foot, bike, bus and skateboard; we know lots of routes through the area and we know how to be safe.*
   - *We have detailed knowledge that is different to that of adults and we use our knowledge differently to them.*
   - *The environment is important to us. We want more wildlife, we want a cleaner and safer environment; we want to care for the environment.*
   - *The local community does not provide things for us to do and places for us to be.*
   - *We are concerned about how well the community provides for minority groups.*

2. **Children have difficulty taking action to achieve what they want for their local environment because they do not know how to go about it.**
3. **Children's knowledge of their local community and ideas to improve their environment are not included in the school curriculum. However, children feel strongly that their schools should support them in achieving their goals.**

Figure 1.   Children's research findings about 10–12 year old children's experience in the local environment and community.

4.   *Developing an ethical approach to the dissemination of children's research findings*

In terms of a research project where children and adults collaborate it would be easy for the adults to take responsibility for dissemination not least because of their greater experience with conventional forms of dissemination such as written reports and papers. Planning how and where dissemination should take place was an ongoing task for the Research Team which agreed on the importance of children's role in this and the impact they could have on both adult and child audiences:

> Involving young people themselves in the dissemination has been shown to have a strong impact on adult audiences. (Bragg 2007, 19)

Consideration was afforded to different forms of dissemination for the range of audiences, not least the children who had been researched (Kirby 2004b, 278).

The dissemination methods employed by the children included:

- Power Point presentations to the school Senior Management Team;
- sending an email to the local Member of Parliament (MP) and later meeting with him;
- giving interviews reported in local newspapers;
- contributing photographs and reports to a regular school newsletter and wall displays;
- planning and implementing a Children's Conference to which 11–12 year old children, teachers and local community officials and academics were invited;
- making and burying 'time capsules' in the school grounds for children and people of the future;
- making a DVD film;[2] including a future scenario acted and filmed in the local park;

- making an oral presentation to a Local Authority conference; and
- leading an open forum discussion with two academic visitors to the University of Bath who separately visited the school.

Three important conditions for children's successful participation in dissemination have therefore emerged through the L2C project experience. These are that:

(i) children's authentic views and words are represented;
(ii) forms of dissemination are concomitant with children's own interests and skills; and
(iii) children play a key role in deciding how and when ideas emerging from the project should be disseminated.

Reflections

In reflecting on the challenges of undertaking participatory research in school settings the over riding and ongoing concern has been to promote children's equal involvement with adults. Given that children had existing relationships with the school-based adults in this project it was difficult for children to move away from their existing compliant role. However, evidence from end of project interviews with children and adults involved in the research suggests that through their involvement the children felt more empowered and skilled to engage in research and contribute to school and local decision making. In addition, the teacher-researchers appreciated children's potential in this respect. The children also had a sense of frustration that, without the project, their potential would not have been realised. The teacher-researchers were keen to embed the project in school life but appreciated the difficulties of extending the principles of participation to the wider community of teachers, adults and children in the school:

> Within the project children are viewed differently, however, outside of the project there's status quo. The project has come so far but there's still much to do to make it a proper reform to transfer across the school. (teacher researcher end of project interview)

A number of other challenges were faced during the L2C research. The emergent nature of the research led to issues around obtaining informed consent to participate as it was not possible to predict to what children were consenting. Furthermore, in developing the research there were tensions between the school agenda and the research agenda, for example, the need for Research Team children to miss lessons to do the research, or to use lesson time to conduct data collection with the year group. Equally, concerns about children's health and safety in undertaking local environment research prevented children using some of the data gathering methods that they had planned.

Nevertheless, there seem to be three positive outcomes from the research experience in terms of children's role in the research. Firstly, the children played a significant role in developing and implementing research methods. They were able to develop 'child friendly' methods that were sensitive to children's environmental experience and that enabled children to express themselves in different ways appropriate to their age and ability. Secondly, the children grew in confidence and capacity as researchers and in decision making. As the research progressed, the children played an increasing role in driving and implementing the research process and the adults' main role became one of support and facilitation; the introduction of older students as 'mentors' seemed to promote children's confidence and independence as researchers and reduce their reliance on adults. Thirdly, through this project the children came to see the value of research; they had a strong desire to share this and their findings with others and had plans to continue their local environment research and take action from this. At the end of the project the children talked in groups about their experience of the project, how it might impact on the school in the future and what else they would like to do:

> I'd like it (L2C) to keep going ... but we should try to get even more involved with our community ... and use the research to try to get a new way of doing it like kids maybe building something inside the school like composting and show it to the adults ... so we can bring change into the community. (Gemma, year 7)

The examples and issues discussed have illustrated the capacity of children as researchers; we believe that the ability of children to do research is vastly underestimated by many adults. From her international literature review of research by children Alderson (2001) concludes how often:

> adult researchers note their surprise at child researchers' competence ... (and) frequently emphasise the value of listening to children, a point that is made more effectively when children can express themselves through doing the relevant research. (151).

We have shown some of the possibilities for researching collaboratively with children in school settings and enabling children's participation in school decision making. These have demonstrated that children might be better placed than adults to undertake research into children's experiences. For such an endeavour to be successful children need the opportunity to be genuine research partners, and not research subjects, and to focus on issues that matter to children.

Notes

1. During Research Team meetings it became evident how much the year 7 children valued their year 12 mentors and so mentors were approached to become involved in L2C; four volunteered. The school has a system of mentoring whereby each tutor group is allocated two year 12 mentors who are given some training; this was initially set up to support children with bullying issues and their role is primarily pastoral.
2. The children made the DVD themselves and this was the children's original idea. The children sought the help of a range of people to make this including representatives from the local Children's Fund, the school IT technician and an older student with experience of acting on television and in the theatre.
3. The final report of the L2C project and some of the other publications arising from this project can be found at http://www.esrcsocietytoday.ac.uk/ESRCInfoCentre/ViewAward Page.aspx?AwardId=2576.

References

Alderson, P. 2000. Children as researchers: The effects of participation rights on research methodology. In *Research with children*, ed. P. Christensen and A. James, 241–57. London: Falmer Press.

Alderson, P. 2001. Research by children. *International Journal of Social Research Methodology* 4, no. 2: 139–53.

Baacke, D. 1985. *Die 13–bis 18–jährigen: Einführung in probleme des jugendalters* [13 to 16 year olds: Introduction to problems of adolescence]. Weinheim: Beltz.

Barratt, R., and E. Barratt Hacking. 2000. Changing my locality: Conceptions of the future. *Teaching Geography* 25, no. 1: 17–21.

Barratt, R., and E. Barratt Hacking. 2008. A clash of worlds: Children talking about their community experience in relation to the school curriculum. In *Participation and learning: Perspectives on education and the environment, health and sustainability*, ed. A. Reid, B.B. Jensen, J. Nikel, and V. Simovska, 285–98. Dordrecht: Springer.

Barratt Hacking, E., W.A.H. Scott, and R. Barratt. 2007. Children's research into their local environment: Stevenson's gap and possibilities for the curriculum. *Environmental Education Research* 13, no. 2: 225–44.

Barratt Hacking, E., W.A.H. Scott, R. Barratt, W. Talbot, D. Nicholls, and K. Davies. 2007. Education for sustainability: Schools and their communities. In *Environmental and geographical education for sustainability: Cultural contexts*, ed. J. Chi-Lee and M. Williams, 123–37. New York: Nova Science Publishers, Inc.

Bragg, S. 2007. *Consulting young people: A review of the literature*. London: Creative Partnerships. http://www.creative-partnerships.com/content/gdocs/cyp.pdf (accessed May 22, 2008).

Bronfenbrenner, U. 1979. *The ecology of human development*. Cambridge, MA: Harvard University Press.

Children's Commissioner for England. n.d. http://www.childrens-commissioner.co.uk/html/aboutus2.html.

Christensen, P., and J. Allison, eds. 2000. *Research with children: Perspectives and practices*. London: Falmer Press.

Clark, J. 2004. Participatory research with children and young people: Philosophy, possibilities and perils. *Action Research Expeditions* 4: 1–18. http://arexpeditions.montana.edu/articleviewer.php?AID=83&PAGE=2 (accessed June 22, 2008).

Clark, J., A. Dyson, N. Meagher, E. Robson, and M. Wootten. 2001. *Young people as researchers: Possibilities, problems and politics*. York: Youth Work Press.

David, M. 2007. Changing the educational climate: Children, citizenship and learning contexts? *Environmental Education Research* 13, no. 4: 425–36.

David, M., R. Edwards, and P. Aldred. 2001. Children and school-based research: 'Informed consent' or 'educated consent'? *British Educational Research Journal* 27, no. 3: 347–65.

De Koning K., and M. Marion. 1996. Participatory research in health: Setting the context. In *Participatory research in health: Issues and experiences*, ed. K. De Koning and M. Martin. London: Zed Books Ltd.

DfES. 2003. *Every child matters*. London: DfES. http://www. everychildmatters.gov.uk/_files/EBE7EEAC90382663E0D5BBF24C99A7AC.pdf (accessed June 22, 2008).

Earth Summit. 2002. http://www.earthsummit2002.org/.

Flutter, J., and J. Rudduck. 2004. *Consulting pupils: What's in it for schools?* London: Routledge Falmer.

Garbarino, J., F. Stott, and Faculty of the Erikson Institute. 1989. *What children can tell us*. San Francisco: Jossey-Bass.

Hart, R.A. 1997. *Children's Participation: The theory and practice of involving young citizens in community development and environmental* care. London: Earthscan.

Heath, S., V. Charles, G. Crow, and R. Wiles. 2004. Informed consent, gatekeepers and go-betweens. Paper presented at the International Association Sixth International Conference on Social Science Methodology, August, in Amsterdam. http://www.sociology.soton.ac.uk/Proj/Informed_Consent/ISA.rtf (accessed April 5, 2008).

Kagan, J. 1994. *The nature of the child*. New York: Basic Books.

Kellett, M. 2005a. *How to develop children as researchers: A step by step guide to the research process*. London: Sage.

Kellett, M. 2005b. Children as active researchers: A new research paradigm for the 21st century? Published online by ESRC National Centre for Research Methods, NCRM/003. http://www.ncrm.ac.uk/publications.

Kirby, P. 2004a. *A Guide to actively involving young people in research: For researchers, research commissioners, and managers*. Hampshire: Involve. http://www.invo.org.uk/pdfs/Involving_Young_People_in_Research_151104_FINAL.pdf (accessed March 24, 2008).

Kirby, P. 2004b. Involving young people in research. In *The New handbook of children's rights, comparative policy and practices*, ed. B. Franklin, 268–84. London: Routledge.

Laws, S., D. Armit, W. Metzendorf, and P. Percival. 1999. *Time to listen: Young people's experiences of mental health services.* Manchester: Save the Children.

Miller, T., and L. Bell. 2002. Consenting to what? Issues of access, gate-keeping and 'informed' consent. In *Ethics in qualitative research*, ed. M. Mauthner, M. Birch, J. Jessop, and T. Miller. London: Sage.

Morrow, V. 1999. 'It's cool ... 'cos you can't give us detentions and things, can you?': Reflections on research with children. In *Time to listen to children*, ed. P. Milner and B. Carolin, London: Routledge.

Morrow, V. 2008. Ethical dilemmas in research with children and young people about their social environments. *Children's Geographies* 6, no. 1: 49–61.

Ofsted. 2007. TellUs2. Questionnaire summary sheet: National, Ofsted. http://www.ofsted. gov.uk/assets/Internet_Content/CSID/files/National_Summary.pdf (accessed February 3, 2007).

Researching children. n.d. http://www.researchingchildren.org/main-goals/index.php?Itemid= 101.

Roe, M. 2007. Feeling 'secrety': Children's views on involvement in landscape decisions. *Environmental Education Research* 14, no. 2: 467–85.

Save the Children. 2004. *So you want to involve children in research?* Sweden: Save the Children.

Sustainable Development Commission. 2007. *Every child's future matters.* London: Sustainable Development Commission. http://www.sd-commission.org.uk/publications/downloads/ECFM_report.pdf (accessed March 25, 2008).

Sustainable schools. n.d. http://www.teachernet.gov.uk/sustainableschools/.

United Nations (UN). 1989. *Convention on the rights of the child.* Office of the UN High Commissioner for Human Rights. http://www.unhchr.ch/html/menu3/b/k2crc.htm (accessed February 15, 2008).

United Nations Children's Fund (UNICEF). 2004. *The state of the worlds' children.* New York: UNICEF.

Van Matre, S. 1979. *Sunship earth: An acclimatization program for outdoor learning.* Martinsville, IN: American Camping Association.

Talk in primary science: a method to promote productive and contextualised group discourse

Martin Braund

Deparment of Educational Studies, University of York, UK

Modelled Discussions About Science (MoDAS), where adults talk together about scientific ideas, procedures and applications, were devised to model and improve the quality of pupils' discussions. Two examples from one of the project schools are examined to see if these aims were fulfilled and to comment on examples of cognitive and social aspects of discourse and argumentation. Successful features of adult modelled talk included the use of clearly signed 'big-D' discourse for example, how adults take turns, signal agreements and disagreements and challenge each other. Analysis of cognitive aspects of pupils' talk showed sophisticated levels of argumentation. Social functions of dialogue were observed particularly with older pupils. The method is also a way of linking industry and school science so that science learning is more authentic.

Introduction

The research described here exemplifies the role educational research can play in teacher development and in illuminating pedagogy associated with collaborative group work. As the approach reported used contexts from industry, the research also provides insights on school-industry links. A new approach to help pupils enhance the quality of their group discussions in science lessons was devised. Modelled Discussions About Science (MoDAS) are a way of using adults talking together to help primary-aged pupils improve their collaborative talk by having good examples to follow and reflect on. Since the research was pragmatic, to inform a training resource, the approach had to have the potential to provide insights on the actions and content of adults' and pupils' discourse so that new users could see the benefits and pitfalls of using MoDAS. The research involved video recording examples of MoDAS and then looking for signs of the adults' discourse moves and signals that might have helped pupils. The conversations of adults, and subsequently of groups of pupils, were transcribed from the recordings and then the main research issue was which method of analysis would be most useful in communicating how to use MoDAS. Below, as in the training materials, examples of adults' and pupils' discourse are presented with reflective commentaries so that readers and users of the materials can judge to what extent the aims of MoDAS and the quality of discussion and argumentation were apparent.

The MoDAS initiative is part of a larger effort to bring about pedagogical change in primary schools in the UK, the Discussions in Primary Science Project (DiPS). Talk between pupils and its role in cognitive and social learning has been the subject of study over a number of years. The seminal work in the UK of Barnes and Todd (1995), Edwards and Mercer (1987), Des-Fountain and Howe (1992) and in the US of Palinscar and Brown (1984) points to the importance of classroom talk in providing, '... worthwhile opportunities [for children] to work together in small groups, making meaning through talk', (Des-Fountain and Howe 1992, 146). In science lessons pupils' talk has particular importance for learning because:

1: Talk in science helps children to *construct* their understanding

Talking together improves critical thinking and helps children to think about their ideas and compare them to the ideas of others including scientists. Talk rather than writing allows children to rehearse their thinking in a collaborative and safe learning environment because, as Barnes points out: 'the flexibility of speech makes it easier for us to try out new ways of arranging what we know' (Barnes 1992, 125).

2: Talk in science helps children have a more realistic view of science

Science knowledge and ideas are constructed and can be challenged and changed as new evidence is produced. This is the basis of scientific endeavour through which scientists, in Neil Mercer's words, use the: 'process of argument ... to establish which "truths" we agree on' (Mercer 2000, 13). In contrast, many children (and adults) think all scientists do is put on white coats and work alone in laboratories. In fact scientists collaborate and talk in communities more than they work at laboratory benches. ***Doing science*** therefore requires ***talking science***.

3: The 21st Century requires scientifically literate citizens

Children today live in a world increasingly dependent on knowing and understanding some science. As adults their decisions will likely involve their health, their living standards, their leisure and ultimately what kind of world they want to live in. Science education in (secondary) schools is changing rapidly to reflect these needs. Since discussion and argument about evidence and issues can advance scientific thinking (Kuhn 1992) and are now increasingly advocated and practised in secondary school science (Osborne, Erduran and Simon 2004), primary children ought to be ready for the consequent changing styles of teaching and learning.

There have been previous efforts to develop talk in primary classrooms. For example, in the early 1990s the work of the National Oracy Project (NOP) in England translated theoretical considerations and research findings into practical classroom actions (see Norman 1992 for a succinct review of the NOP). More recently there have been efforts to enhance group talk in primary schools through 'dialogic teaching' (Alexander 2004) or by teaching to help improve pupils' ability to talk productively in groups (Howe et al. 2007; Dawes, Mercer, and Wegerif 2000). In spite of these efforts, evidence from systematic reviews of international research (Bennett et al. 2004) shows use of group talk activities in science lessons has been at a very low level, particularly when teachers see science as about factual learning rather than including argumentation and discussion of science topics. The approach reported is part of an effort to redress this.

The Discussion in Primary Science (DiPS) project

This two-year project involved 36 primary schools in a Local Authority (LA) in the North East of England. Schools were urban or suburban and mostly took pupils from areas of severe economic and social disadvantage and with low levels of educational achievement (though this was not the case for the school in which the research reported here was carried out). The project was supported by a grant from the AstraZeneca Science Teaching Trust which supports research and Continued Professional Development (CPD) for teachers in science, mainly in the primary sector. Although the focus of the project was in science, outcomes were intended to benefit the whole curriculum. The MoDAS approach described here was part of the second year of the project in which methods and activities were extended to a larger number of schools.

Modelled discussions about science (MoDAS)

Conceptual framework

Theoretical foundations for designing activities, where adults talking together at the beginning of class models discourse that consequently helps learners develop their own talk in science, were:

(1) Gee's concept of 'big D' discourse – through which learners pick up on more than nuances of language in successful talk, i.e. from body language and signals for turn taking, challenges and so on (Gee 1999); and

(2) social learning theory – identifying organisational aspects of purposeful collaborative talk in groups (Wells 1999; Wood 1998).

MoDAS provide spaces in which metadiscoursal skills (Hardman and Beverton 1993) can be developed by learners where reflection on, rather than merely copying, adult discourse plays an important part.

Systematic reviews of the literature on context-based learning in science reveal that real-world, science-technology-society (STS) contexts are attractive to and motivating for learners (Bennett, Hogarth, and Lubben 2003). The Centre for Innovation and Research in Science Education at the University of York has a history of successful school-industry work stimulating productive science lessons in primary schools. For these two reasons the DiPS team decided that adult group talk and the classroom activities that preceded or followed it should be based in contexts drawn from industry close to schools involved in the project, in this case a large chemical plant on the outskirts of the city.

The aims of MoDAS

We saw MoDAS improving pupils' science talk by:

(1) *Modelling productive discourse*: to demonstrate key dialogic moves and cues that help move discussion and argument in new or more productive directions (Alexander 2004; Mercer, Wegerif, and Dawes 1999).

(2) *Modelling construction of meaning*: showing that adults use language and pose questions in ways that elicit and provide explanations to clarify

meanings and establish better understanding of terms, concepts, principles, procedures and theory (Scott, Mortimer, and Aguiar 2006).

(3) *Modelling 'how science works'*: providing a more authentic version of science whereby learners see that ideas and theories are subject to challenge and validation through discussions between scientists rather than being accepted as pre-determined truths. This is part of a component in the English National Curriculum for science often referred to as 'How science works' (DfES 2004, 37–38).

The MoDAS activities

Two examples of MoDAS were developed and researched in one project school. Both drew on contexts at a local chemical plant and involved a planning meeting between adult participants prior to teaching. The first involved pupils in a Y3/4 class (ages 7–9) in discussion about choosing the right gloves to carry out tasks at the chemical plant. Concepts included the, flexibility, porosity and protective properties of materials. The second involved a Y5/6 class (ages 10–11) discussing methods for dealing with excess heat from the chemical plant and deciding which would be most suitable. Concepts included heat transfer and the economic, practical and environmental implications of heat exchange. In both cases the work was spread over two lessons. Pupils were introduced to a specific problem by an industrialist and the class teacher and then practical work was carried out. In the case of *Gloves*, the MoDAS activity took place at the start of the second lesson and involved the 'adults' – the industrialist, class teacher and another teacher – modelling discussion about glove choice for tasks at the chemical plant. In the case of the second example on *Heat exchange*, the main MoDAS took place in plenary class discussion and involved the class teacher, the same industrialist and the author. Figure 1 summarises the components of both lessons that relate to talk activities and specific strategies used to scaffold and support pupils' talk.

The research

Two research questions (RQs) were identified:

> *RQ1:* To what extent are the three modelling intentions of MoDAS represented in adults' modelled talk?
> *RQ1:* To what extent are social and cognitive aspects of discourse evident in adults' modelled talk and pupils' group talk?

Both lessons were videotaped professionally using a single camera and multiple microphones. The recording team was under the direction of an experienced researcher (the author) who took field notes during the lessons. All recordings were transcribed verbatim. The research team considered three types of analysis commonly used in research on classroom discourse:

(1) Qualitative methods: often semi-ethnographic descriptions accompanied by open reflective commentary.
(2) Quantitative methods: for example counting words, phrases or 'key usages' and sometimes correlating features of talk with factors such as pupils' performance in tests.

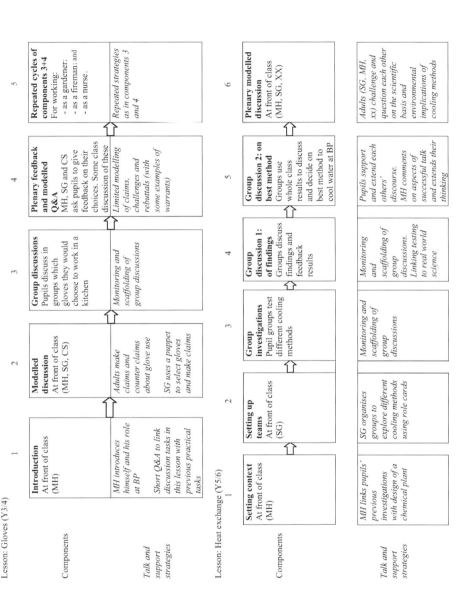

Figure 1.   Modelled Discussions About Science (MoDAS). Lesson components and strategies used to support science talk.

(3) Mixed methods: typically using software to scan talk for 'key usages' and their positions or functions in the discourse.

Since we were interested primarily in describing social and cognitive outcomes and communicating a new approach to teachers and did not wish to count language use or correlate it with other factors such as pupils' performance, we decided on the first of these. Social aspects of pupils' discourse were identified according to the list produced by Barnes and Todd (1995, 27–8). Since most of the dynamic, cognitive aspects of group discourse turned out to be features of argumentation, Toulmin's Argumentation Pattern (TAP), as applied by Erduran, Simon, and Osborne (2004), was used to identify and comment on the occurrence and use of claims, warrants, rebuttals and qualifiers. This application of TAP has the advantage that levels of argumentation, mainly on the basis of the occurrence of warrants and, particularly, rebuttals can be assessed. In Erduran, Simon, and Osborne's (2004) scheme the highest levels of argumentation are those that contain warranted rebuttals to the claims, warrants or backings made by others.

Analysis of and reflection on MoDAS and pupils' discourse

Extracts of transcribed talk are presented for both examples. In the case of *Gloves* the first is from the adults' (modelled) talk and the second from discussion of one group of pupils that followed it. The selection of groups was made on the basis of audibility and practicality for training purposes rather than to be representative of all, or most, group talk that took place. In the style of Barnes and Todd (1995), the extracts below are accompanied by reflective, analytical commentaries.

The Gloves MoDAS

Extract 1: Modelled discussion (about choosing gloves)

In this extract MH is the industrialist from the local chemical works, CS is the class teacher and SG is a second teacher with responsibility for coordinating science in the school. Italicised text shows key physical (Big-D) actions noted from watching the video.

MH: The first job that I did was working in a laboratory. Now I was going to ask what kind of gloves do you think I would wear whenever I was in a laboratory?. 'cos the first thing I wanted to do was to protect my hands but I also needed to be sure I could do the things I needed to do. (*At this point SG places a 'puppet' on her left hand and CS takes a yellow glove with green finger grips*)

CS: (*Turning to face MH and holding up the glove*) Well, I think these gloves are really good because they've got a good grip to them. (*SG's puppet takes a yellow rubber (marigold) glove in 'his' hand*) I think if you were holding things in the laboratory you would have to make sure you didn't drop things if you are holding dangerous chemicals. I think these gloves might be really useful ...

MH: (*Looking at CS*) Well, they would be ... for some things we would do in the laboratory they would be useful, however, (*taking the glove offered by CS*) there is one difficulty with these gloves. (*MH puts one of the gloves on his right hand*) If I had to put my hand inside one of these ... and then if I had to work with a liquid like water (*MH tries to 'wiggle' the fingers of his gloved right hand*) and I had to put my hands inside ... the water would go straight through (*MH turns the gloved hand over*) so they wouldn't keep my hands dry.

SG: (*Speaking through the puppet who holds a yellow rubber, 'marigold'- type, glove in 'his' left hand*) So, these would be OK wouldn't they?

MH: Actually they would ... actually ... they would be much better ... here, can I borrow these ... (*HM reaches across to SG to take the yellow rubber glove from the puppet's hand*)

SG: (*Not 'through' the puppet*) They're flexible ...

MH: These ones are flexible ... (*MH puts the yellow rubber glove on*) and the great thing about these gloves (*MH stretches them to fit*) is that if you were to splash chemicals on your hand ... this would keep the chemicals away from your skin ... so keep your skin safe and protected ... so these are really useful gloves. (*SG's puppet selects another type of glove made of grey coloured suede leather*)
These aren't perfect for every job though and sometimes whenever you are doing things ... with very hot things and you would have to use a very different type of glove.

SG: (*Apparently speaking through the puppet who has an example of the suede glove in 'his' mouth*) So what about these? They are nice and chewy. They are big and strong ... look. (*SG tugs at the glove held by the puppet's mouth*)

MH: They are very strong ... and a bit like what we call gauntlets ...

Commentary

Our first research question (RQ1) was to see to what extent the three aims of MoDAS might be evident in adults' modelled talk. While there were plenty of examples of aim 1, the modelling of productive discourse, there were fewer obvious instances of aims 2 and 3, the construction of meaning and 'How Science Works'. Visual cues such as turning to listen to the person speaking, turn taking and holding or wearing examples of gloves helped anchor spoken meanings. These were useful examples of Gee's 'big-D' discourse and were part of what we had hoped to see. In terms of Barnes and Todd's (1995, 27–8) list of social aspects of productive discourse, which was part of our second research question, we particularly noticed examples of 'modification of others' talk' and 'support for claims others have made by providing evidence'. These social elements provided a *dialogic space* in which productive discussion could take place. For example, this 'space' gave MH an opportunity to warrant, back and qualify his claims about the selection of the yellow, rubber gloves and to provide an authentic example of handling chemicals (an example of our third aim about 'How science works'). In Toulminian, TAP terms, the argumentation could be said to be of a reasonable quality, though there were no real examples of rebuttals which are, according to Erduran, Simon, and Osborne (2004), an indicator of higher level argumentation in science.

At quite an early stage of the discussion, the science coordinator (SG) used a large gloved puppet through which she spoke to support and challenge at various points in the MoDAS. Puppets have been used in England in the last few years to encourage and stimulate classroom discourse (Simon et al. 2008). For example, Simon et al. have found that children, who might not otherwise talk in science lessons, are much more likely to do so when invited to speak by a puppet. In this case the use of the puppet was confusing and a distraction to the MoDAS. For example, towards the end of the MoDAS, the 'puppet' grabbed an example of a glove in his/ her mouth 'claiming' that the glove is, ' ... nice and chewy', not a property of gloves that has anything to do with protection against liquid chemicals or that was the focus of previous exchanges.

Extract 2: An example of pupils' group discourse following the Gloves MoDAS

This is the transcribed talk (where audible) of a group of five pupils, three girls and two boys, invited by MH to discuss which gloves would be best to wear in the kitchen. Comments, related to TAP, have been added (in bold italicised text) after some pupils' utterances.

Girl 1:   (*Reaching to take a pair of gloves from the pile on the desk*) These look good.

Girl 2:   Yeah ... they're stretchy ... big ... (*indistinct*).

Girl 3:   I think them ones (*taking green and yellow gloves with rubberised palms*) ... ' cos you can pick up sharp bits.

(*TAP*) *Warranted claim.*

Boy 1:   (*Reaching to pick a pair of yellow rubber gloves*) Yeah but these rubber gloves .... (*indistinct*) ...

(*TAP*) *Possible example of counter claim or weak rebuttal.*

Girl 3:   (*Trying on a different pair of yellow and blue cloth gloves*) Yeah 'cos a pencil's sharp.

(*TAP*) *Backing her earlier warranted claim.*

Boy 1:   You could wear that (*glove*) and ... then wear that (*i.e. he means wear a large silver gauntlet over the top of the blue-yellow glove*).

(*TAP*) *Qualifying his earlier choice.*

Girl 3:   But how could ya ... go on ... put it on then (*Boy 1 tries on the silver gauntlet but not over the other glove*).

(*TAP*) *Challenging – asking for additional information (social discourse*).

Girl 3:   (*Reaching over to take one of the yellow rubber gloves from boy 1*) They're alright for washing up .... These (*the yellow and blue gloves again*) are ... (*indistinct*) ... for grip ... if you drop a plate.

(*TAP*) *Third warrant for her choice, backed by an example.*

Boy 1:   (*Chooses a green coloured rubber glove*) ... (*recording ends*).

Commentary

In terms of TAP, there was evidence of quite sophisticated argument here, a challenge to those who believe that pupils of this age (7–9) rarely do this. For example, Girl 3 provides three warrants for her selection of glove, the last of which is backed by an example, 'for grip ... if you drop a plate'. Although this extract shows only three of five pupils in the group contributing to discussion, there was evidence on the video recording that participants took turns, listened to each other and reasoned their choices. When the recording was played back to the class teacher (CS), she was impressed with the levels of talk used by these pupils.

The Heat Exchange MoDAS

In this case the modelled discussion took place towards the end of the lesson as a plenary class discussion (see Figure 1). This was not part of the original planning but occurred because discussion was a natural consequence of the sequence of events that preceded it. The group discussions that occurred immediately before the MoDAS had different foci (as shown in Figure 1). The first concentrated on findings from experiments to cool hot water that each group carried out. The second considered results from these experiments and discussion focussed on which method tested by pupils might be best (most practical, economic, efficient) to use to cool water at the chemical plant. There was some modelling, by way of feedback to pupils given by the industrialist (MH) on how effective the first discussions had been, before the second discussion took place. The extract below is from this second round of group discussions.

Extract: An example of pupils' group discourse that preceded the MoDAS

The group comprised two boys and two girls. As before, argumentation features according to TAP are shown where relevant. The 'granny method', referred to by some of the pupils, involved pouring hot water into a container of larger surface area to cool it, therefore like a 'Granny' (Grandmother) might cool hot tea by pouring it from a teacup into a saucer before drinking.

Boy 1:   But also the wind one (*using the natural availability of wind or electric fans*) would be quite good because you're not just using one method (*the 'granny' method*), you're using two, so it gets it done quicker and you're also getting it done, it's cheap.

   (*TAP*) **warranted and backed claim**.

Girl 1:   Yeah, but what if it's not windy enough for the wind to get to the water for it to cool down, so you might not have enough wind to blow it, to cool it down.

   (*TAP*) **challenge and a weak rebuttal to the previous claim adding a qualifier**.

Boy 1:   Yeah, but doing that 'granny' method everyday, it's like you're just doing every method everyday whereas if you use wind then maybe you could like ...

Girl 1:   The 'granny' method is like two (*methods*) in one because you've got the control where you're leaving it and the wind is actually in the air when you're leaving it. So the wind is actually still coming in, you're still spreading it out and you're still leaving it to cool down from the air.

(*TAP*) **Warranted and backed claim.**

Boy 2:   Yeah, but you could just use a fan. You could use a fan to use as the wind.

(*TAP*) **New claim developed from the above.**

Girl 2:   But that's electricity and money.

(*TAP*) **Challenge- rebuttal to new claim of boy 2.**

Boy 1:   Yeah, but if you use the fan, like when it's not windy for a few days, and then the wind when it is windy, and then the 'granny' method also ... get it done quicker.

(*TAP*) **Qualification added to pervious line of reasoning with a warrant**.

MH: (*to the group*) I think the interesting thing for all of us is that you're all right. It sounds a bit strange, but every one of you is right because it depends a little bit on where you find yourself, because every one of the methods that we've talked about had advantages and disadvantages ... . Because your method's quite right (*to girl 1*). It doesn't cost a lot of money. The disadvantage is that you'd need a huge great lake and that might cost a lot of money or take up too much space. And your method's fine, (*to boys 1 and 2*). The one you were talking about together, which is great because you were listening to each other, because you could use the wind on some days and if it wasn't windy you could turn on your fan ... that's actually what we do sometimes. We have a fan assisted cooling tower.

Commentary

As was the case for younger pupils in the *Gloves* MoDAS, the level of argumentation seen here is impressive, particularly as there were examples of warranted and backed claims with some rebuttals. Previous research in science lessons has shown that rebuttals are rare in the argumentation of pupils of a much older age that those studied here (Jimenez-Alexaindre, Rodriguez, and Duschl 2000) and so this observation bodes well for the further development of these pupils' cognitive discourse, if, of course, the pedagogy of the secondary school fosters this (since some of the pupils in this study will soon transfer to secondary school). There is also evidence of some of the more sophisticated social functions of dialogue listed by Barnes and Todd (1995, 27–8) that were missing in the discourse of the younger pupils. For example, Boy 1's premise at the start of the extract that a combination of cooling methods (surface area of water, i.e., the 'granny' method and wind) might be beneficial is picked up and elaborated later by Girl 1 whose utterance clarifies this line of thinking. The development of the idea is taken further in the exchanges between Boys 1 and 2 towards the end of the extract. The point that quality discussion requires quality listening was seized on in the feedback provided by MH that closed the discussion. MH also alluded to the nature of disagreement in combining different viewpoints when he says, 'It sounds a bit strange but every one of you is right because it depends a little bit on where you find yourself . . .'. This was an example consistent with our second aim for MoDAS, modelling 'How science works'. The whole utterance of MH shows a degree of skill in talking with these children and providing reflective feedback on their discourse that many teachers would do well to heed.

Implications of the research

An aim of MoDAS was to promote talk in science as meaning-making and clarification of ideas. Thus MoDAS was intended to use what Barnes and Todd (1995) call 'exploratory talk' whereby pupils engage critically with each others' ideas to help them construct meaning. There is evidence that such activities produce general learning gains, for example in pupils' non-verbal reasoning skills (Howe et al. 2007). This happened in the *Gloves* MoDAS, though the use of another strategy to promote better talk, puppets, may have obscured the direction of discussion and therefore have affected outcomes. The 'constructing meaning' aim of MoDAS was discussed when planning the *Heat exchange* example. However, without the intervention of the author to promote this aspect in the MoDAS that closed the second lesson, the opportunity to address this properly would have been lost. Consequently, it seems there is some work to do in training teachers when using these approaches so that important values of adult modelled talk and their influences on pupils' discourse and consequent learning of science concepts can be maximised.

Field notes revealed organisational features that helped create a purposeful climate for talk. One example was that pupils were given badges related to roles that might occur in collaborative discourse in industry:

Administration Officer – responsible for keeping a written or pictorial record for the group.

Resource Manager – responsible for collecting, setting up and returning all equipment used by the group.

Communications Officer – responsible for collecting the group's ideas and reporting back to the rest of the class.

Personnel Manager – responsible for eliminating disputes within the group and ensuring the team works cooperatively.

It was argued earlier that using contexts from local industry help authenticate science for this age group by locating and relating science ideas in real world examples and there was plenty of evidence of HM doing this, but there is another reason. Research at the university of York shows that pupils of primary school age have few ideas about the nature, processes and job roles of industry (Parvin 1999). So MoDAS and the role badges are further steps in addressing this gap in pupils' wider knowledge and appreciation of industry, as well as helping make abstract ideas more understandable by linking them to local, practical examples.

MoDAS is a tool to be added to teachers' growing pedagogical repertoire through which collaborative group talk can be improved. At this age young brains develop rapidly and talk speeds the rate at which synaptial connections are made (Rose 1997). Yet in England and elsewhere the media continue to berate society for the downturn in talk opportunities amongst children. Watching TV, computer gaming and fewer family meals taken together are frequently cited causes outside the school. In school too there are pressures on time for quality talk in classrooms. The primacy of the written word continues to dominate and is exacerbated by long periods of revision in the run up to national testing at the end of Key Stage 2 (age 11). In secondary science, however, there are at last moves to change teaching away from the drudgery of didacticism towards a more dialogic approach that encompasses discussion and argumentation of ideas and controversies. As in other examples of topic work and practical skills, there may, however, be a pedagogical mismatch if pupils at transfer to secondary school have been used to a completely different approach where collaborative talk has not been part of their experience (Braund 2008). Perhaps the MoDAS approach should have applications at both stages.

Conclusions

As an exercise identifying useful features of MoDAS and pupils' talk in groups to communicate with teachers, who have not experienced the approach, the research has been crucial. It has helped identify video from which to select clips and to devise associated questions and comments for the web-based training resource (see the AstraZencea Science Teaching Trust website). The choice of a qualitative, descriptive-analytical method to reflect on adult and pupils' group discourse was justified. The occurrence of all four aims of MoDAS was encouraging as was the frequency of social discourse and dialogic moves and the quality and levels of argumentation. For the younger age group (7–9) there remains work to be done in helping pupils to work together more productively and collaboratively though what was seen was encouraging. As a way of promoting productive links between industry and schools and in helping authenticate science in schools MoDAS has obvious advantages. Perhaps the final word on the value of talk in human experience should belong to the novelist and essayist Thomas Mann who wrote:

> Speech is civilisation itself. The word, even the most contradictious word, preserves contact – it is silence which isolates. (Thomas Mann 1924, cited in Tripp 1973, 916)

MoDAS and DiPS can be viewed at: http://www.azteachscience.co.uk.

Acknowledgements
The author would like to thank the AstraZencea Science Teaching Trust who funded the DiPS project, teachers in the four project schools who helped produce MoDAS activities, Martin Hegarty at BP Chemicals, Kingston-upon Hull and Tanya Shields, DiPS and CIEC Advisory Teacher.

References
Alexander, A. 2004. *Towards dialogic teaching*. York: Dialogos.
Barnes, D. 1992. The role of talk in learning. In *Thinking voices: The work of the National Oracy Project*, ed. K. Norman, 123–28. London: Hodder and Stoughton.

Barnes, D., and F. Todd. 1995. *Communication and learning revisited*. London: Heinemann.

Bennett, J., S. Hogarth, and F. Lubben. 2003. A systematic review of the effects of context-based and Science-Technology-Society (STS) approaches in the teaching of secondary science. In *Research evidence in education library*. London: EPPI-centre, Social Science Research Unit, Institute of Education.

Bennett, J., F. Lubben, S. Hogarth, B. Campbell, and A. Robinson. 2004. A systematic review of the nature of small-group discussions in science teaching aimed at improving students' understanding of evidence. In *Research evidence in education library*. London: EPPI-Centre, Social Science Research Unit, Institute of Education.

Braund, M. 2008. *Starting science ... again?* London: Sage Publications.

Dawes, L., N. Mercer, and R. Wegerif. 2000. *Thinking together: A programme of activities for developing thinking skills at KS2*. Birmingham: Questions Publishing Company.

Department for Education and Skills (DfES). 2004. *The National Curriculum for England: Science*. London: Department for Education and Skills.

Des-Fountain, J., and A. Howe. 1992. Pupils working together on understanding. In *Thinking voices: The work of the National Oracy Project*, ed. K. Norman, 146–58. London: Hodder and Stoughton.

Edwards, D., and N. Mercer. 1987. *Common knowledge: The development of understanding in the classroom*. London: Methuen/Routledge.

Erduran, S., S. Simon, and J. Osborne. 2004. TAPping into argumentation: Developments in the application of Toulmin's argumentation pattern for studying science discourse. *Science Education* 88, no. 6: 915–33.

Gee, J.P. 1999. *An introduction to discourse analysis theory and method*. London: Routledge.

Hardman, F., and S. Beverton. 1993. Co-operative group work and the development of metadiscoursal skills *Support for Learning* 8, no. 4: 146–50.

Howe, C., A. Tolmie, A. Thurston, K. Topping, D. Christie, K. Livingston, E. Jessiman, and C. Donaldson. 2007. Group work in elementary science: Towards organisational principles for supporting pupil learning. *Learning and Instruction* 17: 549–63.

Jimenez-Aleixandre, M., A. Rodriguez, and R. Duschl. 2000. 'Doing the lesson' or 'doing science': Argument in high school genetics. *Science Education* 84, no. 6: 757–92.

Kuhn, D. 1992. Thinking as argument. *Harvard Educational Review* 62: 155–78.

Mercer, N. 2000. *Words and minds*. London: Routledge.

Mercer, N., R. Wegerif, and L. Dawes. 1999. Children's talk and the development of reasoning in the classroom. *British Educational Research Journal* 25, no. 1: 95–111.

Norman, K., ed. 1992. *Thinking voices: The work of the National Oracy Project*. London: Hodder and Stoughton.

Osborne, J., S. Erduran, and S. Simon. 2004. *Ideas and evidence and argument in science (IDEAS PROJECT)*. London: Kings College, University of London.

Palinscar, A.S., and A.L. Brown. 1984. Reciprocal teaching of comprehension-fostering and comprehension monitoring activities. *Cognition and Instruction* 1: 117–75.

Parvin, J. *Children challenging industry: The research report*. York: University of York.

Rose, C. 1997. *Accelerated learning for the 21st century*. London: Piatkus.

Scott, P., E. Mortimer, and O. Aguiar. 2006. The tension between authoritative and dialogic discourse: A fundamental characteristic of meaning making interactions in high school science lessons. *Science Education* 90: 605–31.

Simon, S., S. Naylor, B. Keogh, J. Maloney, and B. Downing. 2008. Puppets promoting engagement and talk in science. *International Journal of Science Education* 30, no. 9: 1229–48.

Tripp, R.T. 1973. *The international thesaurus of quotations*. Harmondsworth: Penguin Books, George Allen and Unwin.

Wells, G. 1999. *Dialogic enquiry: Towards a sociocultural practice and theory of education*. Cambridge: Cambridge University Press.

Wood, D. 1998. *How children think and learn*. Oxford: Blackwell.

Using qualitative research strategies in cross-national projects: the English–Finnish experience

Graham Vulliamy[a] and Rosemary Webb[b]

[a]Department of Educational Studies, University of York, UK; [b]School of Education, University of Manchester, UK

Some methodological issues are discussed that arise from our comparative research conducted since the early 1990s into primary schooling in Finland and England. This research has been identified as part of a 'new' comparative education that uses qualitative research strategies and which prioritises sensitivity to cultural context in data collection and analysis. The procedures used in our research are considered. Several challenges for cross-national qualitative research are addressed – particularly in relation to language and data analysis. In conclusion brief examples from the findings illustrate how the research approach enabled a comparison between national policy intentions and school outcomes.

Introduction

One of the consequences of the increasingly globalised world in which we live has been that the last two decades have witnessed a burgeoning of interest by educationalists in the educational systems of other countries. It has become evident that the educational policies in many countries have been driven by the same pressures associated with a market-driven, low-tax, neo-liberal economic idcology. Moreover, changes in the global organisation of work result in countries seeing themselves as in competition with each other for the production of highly skilled and flexible workers. Thus the quality of national educational systems shaping the workforce is compared internationally in surveys and the results of these increasingly determine policy-makers' agendas.

In the following sections we reflect on some methodological issues arising from two comparative research projects we have conducted since the early 1990s into primary schooling in Finland and England. We are currently engaged in a third small-scale project but concentrate here on research that is completed. In retrospect, the original serendipitous choice of Finland for such comparative research has been a fortuitous one in that, firstly, subsequent international test surveys have seen this country consistently top the international league tables (Välijärvi et al. 2007) and, secondly, Finland provides a vivid example of the cultural mediation of global policies at national and local level.

In the early 1990s a number of fundamental changes in Finnish national education policy and governance were introduced. While these have been interpreted as a response to global pressures such as marketisation, managerialism and business-style accountability, they have been filtered through a peculiarly Nordic welfare state tradition that had always put a high premium on the goal of equality (Rinne et al. 2002). As in England, financial powers and decision-making were delegated from national and local levels to schools. However, while the 1988 Education Reform Act (ERA) in England introduced a statutory highly prescriptive national curriculum, constructivist theories of learning led Finland to implement a *New Framework Curriculum for the Comprehensive School* (National Board of Education 1994) and move away from centrally prescribed national curricula towards the development of school-based curricula with active learning pedagogies (Norris et al. 1996). Setting out its case for 'modernising the teaching profession' the New Labour government claimed that: 'The time has long gone when isolated unaccountable professionals made curriculum and pedagogical decisions alone without reference to the outside world' (DfEE 1998, 14). By contrast the rhetoric of Finnish national policy was of emancipating teachers from existing constraints and giving them ownership over curriculum development in their schools.

Our research has taken two broad approaches, both of which are underpinned by a qualitative research methodology. The first approach, used in the York-Finnish Project (YFP), involved a comparison of six ethnographic case studies of primary schools in each country. The second, in the York-Jyväskylä Teacher Professionalism (YJTP) project, involved a comparative analysis of samples of semi-structured interviews from primary school teachers in each country. The rationale for such approaches, to be discussed more fully in the next section, stems from a dissatisfaction with more traditional methodologies in comparative education. Consequently our research has been identified as part of a 'new' comparative research tradition 'developing innovative methodologies in order to undertake studies which take account of tradition, context and national and local education policy' (Troman and Jeffrey 2005, 207).

Comparative education and the policy-practice interface

The adoption of a qualitative methodology for our comparative research was informed by earlier arguments (Crossley and Vulliamy 1984; Vulliamy, Lewin, and Stephens 1990) that the literature on comparative education had hitherto been too dominated by, on the one hand, a combination of discussion of national policies and system-wide features and, on the other, by the results of large-scale quantitative surveys. By focussing on the processes of schooling and on teachers' and pupils' perspectives, qualitative research methods can penetrate the policy-practice interface and this is especially important in the evaluation of educational innovations. The results of traditional quantitative input-output research designs are often difficult for readers to interpret because they assume, firstly, that the adopted policy is actually implemented and, secondly, that this process of implementation corresponds to the policy directive itself. To have a good chance of success, educational policies or innovations, whether initiated by national policy makers or by international organisations, need to be in tune with the everyday realities of the classroom and the motivations and capabilities of ordinary teachers. However, traditional large-scale research projects often fail to address these. Through their concern with the everyday practices of teachers and pupils, qualitative methods are alert to the unintended consequences of innovation and can identify unforeseen constraints or facilitating factors that may emerge at the grass roots level of individual schools and classrooms. As argued by Fullan, 'neglect of the phenomenology of change – that is, how people actually experience change as distinct from how it might have been intended – is at the heart of the spectacular lack of success of most social reforms' (1982, 4).

The last two decades have witnessed widespread and profound changes in primary schooling in both Finland and England brought about through the pressures of globalisation. Ball has argued that an understanding of such processes should 'address the processes of translation and recontextualisation involved in the realization or enactment of policy in specific national and local settings' (1998, 119). One research strategy for this is policy ethnography which assumes that 'policy *as* practice is "created" in a trialectic of dominance, resistance and chaos/freedom' (Ball 1994, 11) and that struggles between competing discourses play an important part in this creation. Such an approach has been used in studies of the implementation in schools of national reforms (e.g. Bowe, Ball, and Gold 1992) and in the impact of such reforms on teacher identity (e.g. Welmond 2002). However, with very few exceptions (e.g. Broadfoot et al. 1993; Alexander 2000), comparative research on policy across different countries tends to be restricted to discussions of the influences of globalisation on national policies (e.g. Gordon and Whitty 1997; Taylor et al. 1997; Klette 2002) rather than on the 'policy as practice' that necessitates the analysis of data collected from those teachers on whose work practices such policies impact. The research design for the YFP, conducted between 1994 and 1996, was an early attempt to remedy this relative neglect.

In this article we will discuss, first, the methods used in our research – together with some methodological issues arising from these methods – and then some of the substantive findings emanating from it.

Research methods

The YFP investigated the processes of curriculum change in primary schools in England and Finland during the period 1994-1996. This comparison had a special interest because in many respects the educational policies of the two countries were moving in opposite directions (Webb et al. 1998; Webb and Vulliamy 1999a,b). The principal aim of the YFP was to examine the effect of the national policy changes on the nature, planning and teaching of the curriculum and the processes involved in the management of change within primary schools in each country. Given the project's focus on the implementation of policy in practice, a qualitative research strategy was adopted with in-depth case studies of six English schools from four local authorities (using a team of three English researchers) and six Finnish schools from four local municipalities (using a team of five Finnish researchers).

While utilizing a questionnaire would have enabled a much larger sample, earlier research on the implementation of the National Curriculum in English primary schools (Webb and Vulliamy 1996) had suggested that a questionnaire survey would be inappropriate. Many of the terms that would have been necessary in such a questionnaire – such as 'group work', 'integrated day', 'setting' and 'topic work' – were either ambiguous or used in totally different ways in different English schools, quite apart from the additional problems of linguistic and conceptual equivalence to the Finnish context to which we refer in the next section. Also, the complexity of curricular organisation and planning in various schools was such that researchers could only comprehend it if given the opportunities for detailed questioning about such approaches, referring to documents *in situ* with teachers themselves. Access to classrooms was also important to establish the contexts in which policies were to be implemented and to consider the effects of plans and policies on practice.

Fieldwork in each country combined the use of longitudinal case studies (6 of the 12 schools) – varying in length from data collection over a two-year period to that over a 16-month period – with shorter, more focused case studies taking place within a single term. The longitudinal studies typically began with an intensive one-week period of observation being followed by about three separate day visits per term for the remaining four or five terms. In some of the schools, particularly the smaller ones (see Vulliamy et al. 1997), classroom observation and teacher interviews were supplemented by interview data from other relevant personnel such as parents, governors, non-teaching assistants, clerical and ancillary staff, and pupils. Initial analysis of the data, which consisted of transcriptions of tape-recorded interviews, fieldnotes and documents, used a process of category generation and saturation, based upon the 'constant comparison' method originally advocated by Glaser and Strauss (1967). Emerging findings were then further analysed by reference to the literature on teacher identity, the management of change, teacher professionalism and globalization.

The aim of the YJTP project 2001–2002 follow-up study was to address the question as to how the primary school teachers in each country construed the policy changes they were being required to make in terms of their perceptions of teaching as a profession. We decided to re-interview all those teachers who in the year 2001 were still teaching in their original YFP schools and some teachers from the original sample who had left (either to new teaching posts, to other jobs or to retirement). Also, in each country, one headteacher/principal who was newly appointed to a sample school and had therefore not been interviewed in the original study was interviewed in order to be able to provide relevant contextual details of changes in that school since the earlier YFP research. This gave a comparative sample of 24 English and 13 Finnish teachers (see Webb et al. 2004a, for details of the sample). The teacher interviews lasted between 40 and 70 minutes and used a semi-structured interview schedule that had been designed collaboratively with the Finnish researchers. Each of the interviews was fully transcribed and the Finnish ones were translated into English.

The analysis used the same approach as that adopted in the YFP. However, unlike the earlier research, the depth and rigour of the analysis of the teacher interviews was aided by the use of winMAX (and its successor MAXqda) software for qualitative data analysis. A major advantage of such software is that it enables a single complete archive file to contain all texts, category/codings and analytic memos, thus providing an audit trail of the analysis process. It is especially helpful for a cross-national research project because such files can easily be sent by email, enabling an ongoing process of email communication concerning the precise manner in which segments of interview transcripts have been coded and subsequently analysed.

Working on joint projects with researchers from Finland has many benefits in terms of knowledge exchange and providing a fresh perspective on English data, so making the familiar strange and generating new insights and ideas. However, as Osborn (2004) argues, cross-cultural research provides particular methodological challenges and, as Troman and Jeffrey (2005, 2007) suggest, these are exacerbated by the use of qualitative strategies in such comparative studies. Next we consider some of the lessons learned from our own experience.

The challenges of cross-national research

Commenting on the main limitations of their evaluation of the Finnish comprehensive school reform conducted using day visits to 50 schools, an English research team noted that:

> The most obvious and significant limitation of the evaluation is that none of the team spoke Finnish. This one fact alone made some aspects of the fieldwork extremely time consuming and frustrating. It is a testimony to the strength of language teaching in Finland that it was possible for us to do this kind of evaluation at all. Sometimes we had to work through translation, but mostly we worked directly in English. Where translation was needed the team were provided with excellent translators who worked extremely hard on our behalf. The need for translation, however, did limit the length and depth of interviews and observations, and as ever it made understanding more difficult. Our own lack of Finnish made it difficult to explore nuance of meaning and made classroom observation more restricted than it would normally be. (Norris et al. 1996, 4)

In the YFP we had the advantage that, with Finnish researchers researching their own schools, such problems of lack of understanding of the Finnish schools did not ensue. However, despite the fact that all five members of the Finnish research team spoke English (and some had experience also of writing in English), the issues of language differences posed a number of problems. The 'time consuming and frustrating' nature of communication and translation occurred for us, not at the point of data collection, but at the point of data analysis.

The first of such language issues was that the differing cultural contexts of schooling in the two countries resulted in certain words having very different meanings within the two systems. The first stages of comparative analysis took place at a week-long meeting in Jyväskylä in 1995 between the three-person English and five-person Finnish research teams. This meeting involved discussion of the case-study research which had already taken place. At that stage detailed case records had been produced for six schools – three from each country – based on the first ten months fieldwork. Following a collaborative 'brainstorming' session to elucidate the key themes arising from the research to date, suggestions were made as to the likely contents of a final comparative report to be written in English. At this meeting it was some time before the English researchers recognised that when the Finnish researchers used the term 'evaluation' essentially they were referring to 'assessment' in English terminology. Similarly, concepts such as 'whole class teaching' or 'group work' meant very different things in the two countries. At one level this reflects a general problem, frequently commented upon by qualitative researchers, that language is always context specific and that even within different schools within the same country or geographical area, terms can convey very different meanings. At another level, however, it reflects the more deep-seated problem, often referred to by cross-national researchers (see, e.g., Pergnier 1978; Lewin 1990; Osborn 2004) that there may be a lack of conceptual equivalence between different cultures with different languages – for example, Broadfoot et al. (1993) note how 'in the Bristaix study "accountability" has no equivalent meaning in French and therefore the expression "professional responsibility" was chosen, since it appeared to have validity in both countries' (48).

The second major language issue, discussed in Webb et al. (1998), was that the English researchers, who were to write the comparative report and then amend it in the light of the Finnish researchers' comments, did not have direct access to all the data that the Finnish researchers had collected. Here a decision was made that much of the generous funding by Finnish organisations for the research should be spent on translating in a non-polished form, not only the Finnish researchers' case records, but those parts of data of particular interest to the English researchers following their preliminary comparative analysis. Thus, at a relatively late stage of the comparative analysis process, requests were made for translations of data on specific themes, such as one school's collation and use of parental responses to a questionnaire which teachers had given them as part of the school's self-evaluation strategy.

An unconventional aspect of the YFP, which arises partly from the fact that the English researchers do not speak or read Finnish, is that separate English and Finnish analyses were encouraged resulting in additional project publications and dissemination rather than trying to reach a cross-culturally agreed focus and/or theoretical interpretation of all the data. While rigorous attempts were made to confirm the accuracy of the Finnish data (including agreement on their first-order interpretations), it is recognised that such data are sometimes presented within a context of substantive literature that was unfamiliar to the Finnish project team. The obverse of this is also the case. Detailed case records of all six English school case studies were made available to the Finnish project team in order that they could write joint publications in Finnish (e.g. Hämäläinen et al. 1999), which, while utilising English data, could do this with reference to theoretical frameworks and substantive literatures to which the English team did not have access because they were only available in Finnish. While some of these literatures address ideas and perspectives derived from Finnish culture and educational traditions, others are based upon theoretical frameworks enjoying considerable currency in England. However, in a Finnish setting and interacting with Finnish literatures, such theories take on particular cultural perspectives and meanings. For example, constructivism, which offers the Finnish researchers particular ways of understanding teacher learning and attitudes to change, is used differently from related contexts in England, such as in research on primary teachers' responses to science INSET (Summers and Kruger 1994).

As Troman and Jeffrey (2007) note, cross-national comparative research brings particular problems concerning the standardisation of data collection and analysis. One of the criticisms made of the 'old' comparative education is that the quantitative research strategies that they adopt – such as large-scale survey methods and standardised achievement tests – are unable to take culture fully into account (Osborn 2004). Advocates of the 'new' comparative education, for which sensitivity to cultural context is viewed as a hallmark, have used a variety of approaches on a continuum from the mixed-methods (questionnaires and interviews) to be found in, for example, Osborn's (2001) research into secondary schooling in England, France and Denmark to comparative ethnographic school case studies as in the YFP discussed above or the later research by Troman and Jeffrey (2005, 2007) in the *Creative Learning and Student Perspectives* (CLASP) Project in ten European countries. Both the YFP and CLASP projects utilised the wide range of qualitative research methods (but particularly observation and interviews) to be found in ethnography. The YJTP project might be viewed as at an intermediary point on the continuum. Given that the research questions enquired into teachers' perspectives on professionalism, rather than having research questions focused upon both perspectives and actions as in the preceding YFP, we saw no need for an ethnographic approach that included observation. However, to avoid the problems of over standardisation associated with questionnaire surveys, we used qualitative semi-structured interviews and, to preserve a strong sense of cultural context, drew these from teachers in the same schools for which we already had ethnographic data.

As Troman and Jeffrey (2007) argue, the use of a common semi-structured interview schedule builds in a degree of prior standardisation to the analysis that is not possible with a comparative ethnographic approach (where in both the YFP and CLASP projects the final comparative report was written on the basis of a 'qualitative synthesis' of various researchers' case-study reports). However, it is somewhat misleading for them to suggest in their discussion of our cross-cultural qualitative data analysis procedures, that this necessarily eased our problems of data analysis by enabling us to control 'data production, analysis and interpretation' (Troman and Jeffrey 2007, 515). We made explicit in our article that 'the English data [for the YJTP project] were coded by the English researchers but the Finnish data were coded by the English researchers in collaboration with the Finnish team at a week-long meeting in Jyväskylä in July 2002' (Webb et al. 2004a, 89). Given this, it is difficult to see how Troman and Jeffrey received the impression that 'the researchers who carried out the interviews did not carry out the initial categorisation, but kept the involvement of research personnel down to two' (514). As with the analysis, the design of the semi-structured interview schedule was also done collaboratively between the two research teams. In fact, we would argue that the week-long meetings held in Jyväskylä for both the YFP and YJTP project played the same vital role in providing a framework for a 'shared repertoire' that Troman and Jeffrey (2005) identify as essential to the workings of their CLASP project.

The relationship between research approach and project findings

The findings of both the YFP and YJTP projects contribute to the ongoing debate concerning the extent to which global trends lead to homogeneity in educational systems or a 'glocalised response' (Robertson 1995). As shown by our data, such a glocalised response is derived not only from different cultural mediations at the national policy level but also from the various innovation biographies of different schools and the experience and values of the different English headteachers and Finnish principals. In this section a few key findings on the impact of education reform on primary teachers and their classroom practice are outlined in order to illustrate some of the ways in which the chosen research approach enabled a comparison between national policy intentions and intended and unintended outcomes at school level in each country. First is an example of how the different political, cultural and educational contexts of the two countries have given rise to contrasting policies on the curriculum and pedagogy but which generate markedly similar responses from teachers. Second is an example of converging policy recommendations in relation to teachers working collaboratively that have resulted in similar responses despite different cultural contexts. Third is an example of how contrasting national policies in relation to the global demands for accountability have had crucial differential effects on school cultures and teachers.

Contrasting policies generating similar responses

In the 1990s curriculum and pedagogical reform moved in opposite directions yet teachers in both countries experienced burgeoning workloads and stress. In Finland teachers were required to plan a curriculum for their schools and to consider introducing the 'active-learning' approaches promoted by national policy – ideally characterised by: direct experiences; investigations and problem-solving; collaborative small-group work and pupil ownership of learning (Niemi and Kohonen 1995). In the two Finnish schools that were already experimenting with the kinds of practice advocated by the reforms, for most teachers the government rhetoric of empowerment became a reality. They were very enthusiastic about the changes and enjoyed being at the forefront of valued practice. However, for teachers in the other four schools the freedom provided by the new curriculum requirements generated considerable insecurity as they were unsure what was expected of them and unfamiliar with the processes involved in curriculum development. They began to experience the same kinds of work intensification and anxiety reported by the English teachers implementing the National Literacy and National Numeracy strategies and more usually associated with 'behaviourally prespecified curricula, repeated testing, and strict and reductive accountability systems' (Apple 1986, 43). Thus both English and Finnish teachers felt deskilled and their experience devalued by education reform.

Six years later the negative effects of reform had further taken its toll on the project teachers in both countries. In England morale was low and having an increasingly detrimental effect on the recruitment and retention of teachers although the publication of the Primary National Strategy (DfES 2003) with its possibility for greater curricular freedom began to restore teachers' self-confidence. In Finland teachers increasingly questioned the necessity and value of the extra work involved in schools devising their own curriculum leading to support for the introduction of the National Core Curriculum for Basic Education (National Board of Education 2004). This outlined content and specified lesson hours for each grade to which the municipalities could add their own specifications.

Similar policies with similar responses

Collaborative working involving teamwork in schools, networking between schools and collaboration with the wider community are advocated in both countries as the way forward for raising standards and promoting innovation in primary schools (DfES 2003; MoE 2007). In England since the ERA (1988), largely as a result of teachers working together to implement government reform particularly in relation to planning the National Curriculum, the individualised culture of primary schools has changed to one where collegiality is the norm, although the pace of change and pressures of accountability mean that teachers may be 'collaborating under constraint' (Woods et al. 1997). The project teachers were critical of the escalating numbers of meetings with colleagues, governors and parents that diminished time for class preparation and other aspects of their role including informal sharing with colleagues. Since 2005 further opportunities for working together have opened up as all primary teachers with timetabled teaching commitments have a contractual entitlement to guaranteed planning, preparation and assessment (PPA) time within the timetabled teaching day. Where PPA time has been organised to release staff within a key stage, or in larger schools within a year group, at the same time this has enabled staff not only to plan together but to develop practice (Webb and Vulliamy, forthcoming).

In Finland, although over many years numerous studies and teachers' manuals have advocated the development of a shared pedagogic culture and a stronger sense of community, moving towards this has been a slow process (Huusko et al. 2007). Prior to curriculum reform in 1994 Finnish primary teachers were unaccustomed to joint planning and curriculum decision-making. In the larger project schools initially this was experienced as a stressful process because it revealed different values and preferred practices and then, as it became established, resented for taking up too much of teachers' time and energy. However, as in England, collaborative planning has now become the norm. Finnish teachers are required to 'participate for three hours a week in the school's joint instructional planning, in subject group and issue-group meetings, in school-home cooperation and in tasks related to instructional planning and development of school work' (MoE 2007, 22). Generally attitudes in the project schools towards such joint planning were positive, especially among the younger teachers.

Different policies giving rise to different responses

English project teachers described the unremitting pressure on themselves and pupils exerted by the government's standards agenda through the mechanisms of high stakes national tests, the setting and meeting of attainment targets, league tables of performance, OFSTED inspections and performance management. As a result of such excessive surveillance and control, as one headteacher put it:

> It is as if nobody trusts your professionalism any more – you know what you say and your judgement. You constantly have to justify your judgement and I think that is one of the most tiresome things about the whole process of change that we are constantly having to justify ourselves, constantly having to demonstrate we are doing the job. (Head of a small school)

The situation in which English teachers find themselves is in marked contrast to that of Finnish teachers. The only national testing in Finland is the matriculation examination that concludes upper secondary school. Pupils received reports twice during the year and the assessments given on these were derived from achievement in class, homework and tests organised by teachers. National standards are monitored by the National Board of Education, which administers tests to pupils in the sixth and ninth grade in a sample of schools each Spring. The sample schools receive their test results but these are not made publically available. The extremely negative impact that OFSTED inspections can have on teachers' work, professional identity and health was documented in the YFP (Webb et al. 1998). In Finland the national system of inspections was transferred to a province-based system in the 1970s and this was discontinued in 1991. In the context of decentralisation and deregulation, one of the central objectives of the *New Framework Curriculum for the Comprehensive School* (National Board of Education 1994) was to develop school self-evaluation involving both teachers and parents to ensure continuous review and development at school level. While in the project schools self-evaluation appeared to have considerable limitations, 'schools had ownership over their methods of data collection and analysis and commitment to respond to evaluation findings which led to direct and immediate changes to practice' (Webb et al. 1998, 554). However, a follow-up study found the initial enthusiasm had dissipated with self-evaluation described as having 'become like a merry-go-round that has to be run beside everything else' with no time to address the issues raised (Webb et al. 2004a).

Finnish teachers have long enjoyed a high level of trust in their proficiency and capacity to fulfil curricular aims (Sahlberg 2007). While the success of Finnish pupils in international surveys of achievement is attributed to a range of interrelated factors, teachers' expertise and professionalism are regarded as making a major contribution (Välijärvi et al. 2007). This recognition at both national and local level boosts their self-image and job satisfaction:

> I view this as a good job. It involves trust from the state and the municipality in relation to the curriculum and the operational framework. They show a certain trust that schools can do things appropriately – perhaps not always in the best possible way – but they trust teachers' and schools' professional competence. I am really happy in my work. (Principal of a small school)

The status of teachers is high and primary teaching one of the most popular professions for young people (MoE 2007).

Questions posed

The above brief extracts from our project findings raise interesting questions about the future direction and impact of education reform in both countries for further consideration in our ongoing joint English/Finnish research:

- How far will England reduce the control on teachers exerted through the National Curriculum, national testing and accountability measures?
- In a climate of shrinking resources can Finland sustain an approach based on equality of opportunity at an operational level as its population becomes more diverse and makes additional demands on schools?
- If Finland loses its place at the top of the international surveys of attainment will teachers continue to enjoy the trust in their competence manifest in the lack of constraining accountability systems or will they become subject to increasing controls?
- Will the two countries move closer together in their policy formation, implementation and teachers' experiences or will their distinctive cultural contexts and educational traditions ensure that fundamental differences remain?

Conclusion

We have described the qualitative research methods used in two comparative research projects that we conducted in England and Finland and have discussed the specific issues we encountered in researching in two countries with different languages and different cultures. The research findings reveal not only the ways in which qualitative data can portray teachers' experiences and perceptions of government reform and identify the differences between government rhetoric and lived reality, but also the value of such data for comparative purposes. The power of global trends in education to affect fundamentally the lives and work of teachers internationally is demonstrated. However, also revealed in detail are the ways in which through the processes of 'glocalisation' trends are interpreted as a result of a nation's history, culture and values. In addition to new knowledge and understandings of the educational systems and the process of change in each country, the research projects enabled the researchers to learn from one another and develop fresh insights into the nature and the possibilities of the research methods employed.

Acknowledgements

We should like to thank all the Finnish researchers at the University of Jyväskylä with whom we have worked but especially Seppo Hämäläinen (Emeritus Professor of Teacher Education) and Anneli Sarja (Senior Researcher and Adjunct Professor in the Institute for Educational Research) without whom the research projects reported here would not have been possible.

References

Alexander, R. 2000. *Culture and pedagogy, international comparisons in primary education.* Oxford: Blackwell Publishers Ltd.
Apple, M. 1986. *Teachers and texts: A political economy: A political economy of class and gender relations in education.* New York: Routlege and Kegan Paul.
Ball, S.J. 1994. *Education reform: A critical and post-structural approach.* Buckingham: Open University Press.
Ball, S.J. 1998. Big policies/small world: An introduction to international perspectives in education policy. *Comparative Education* 34, no. 2: 119–30.
Bowe, R., S.J. Ball, and A. Gold. 1992. *Reforming education and changing schools: Case studies in policy sociology.* London: Routledge.
Broadfoot, P., M. Osborn, M. Gilly, and A. Bûcher. 1993. *Perceptions of teaching: Primary school teachers in England and France.* London: Cassell.
Crossley, M., and G. Vulliamy. 1984. Case-study research methods and comparative education. *Comparative Education* 20: 193–207.
Department for Education and Employment (DfEE). 1998. *Teachers: Meeting the challenge of change.* London: Stationery Office.
Department for Education and Skills (DfES). 2003. *Excellence and enjoyment, a strategy for primary schools.* London: DfES.
Fullan, M. 1982. *The meaning of educational change.* Toronto: OISE Press.
Glaser, B., and A. Strauss. 1967. *The discovery of Grounded Theory.* Chicago: Aldine.
Gordon, L., and G. Whitty. 1997. Giving the 'hidden hand' a helping hand? The rhetoric and reality of neoliberal education reform in England and New Zealand. *Comparative Education* 33, no. 3: 453–67.
Hämäläinen, S., E. Kimonen, R. Nevalainen, M. Nikki, G. Vulliamy, and R. Webb. 1999. Opettaja opetussuunnitelman muutosprosessin toteuttajana: Muuttuako vai ei muuttua? Jyväskylän yliopisto. Opettajankoulutuslaitos. *Opetuksen Perusteita Ja Käytänteitä* 34: 107–16.
Huusko, J., J. Pietarinen, K. Pyhältö, and T. Soini. 2007. *Yhtenäisyyttä rakentava peruskoulu – yhtenäisen perusopetuksen ehdot ja mahdollisuudet.* [Towards an undivided comprehensive school]. Turku: Suomen Kasvatustieteellinen seura.
Klette, K. 2002. Reform policy and teacher professionalism in four Nordic countries. *Journal of Educational Change* 3: 265–82.
Lewin, K. 1990. Data collection and analysis in Malaysia and Sri Lanka. In *Doing educational research in developing countries: Qualitative strategies*, ed. G. Vulliamy, K. Lewin, and D. Stephens. London: Falmer Press.
Ministry of Education, Finland. 2007. *Improving school leadership, Finland country background report.* Finland: Ministry of Education.

National Board of Education. 1994. *New Framework Curriculum for the Comprehensive School.* Finland: National Board of Education.

National Board of Education. 2004. *National Core Curriculum for Basic Education.* Finland: National Board of Education.

Niemi, H., and V. Kohonen. 1995. *Towards new professionalism and active learning in teacher development: Empirical findings on teacher education and induction.* Tampere: University of Tampere.

Norris, N., R. Aspland, B. MacDonald, J. Schostak, and B. Zamoski. 1996. *An independent evaluation of comprehensive curriculum reform in Finland.* Helsinki: National Board of Education.

Osborn, M. 2001. Constants and contexts in pupil experience of learning and schooling: Comparing learners in England, France and Denmark. *Comparative Education* 37, no. 3: 267–78.

Osborn, M. 2004. New methodologies for comparative research? Establishing 'constants' and 'contexts' in educational experience. *Oxford Review of Education* 30, no. 2: 265–85.

Pergnier, M. 1978. Language-meaning and message meaning: Towards a sociolinguistic approach to translation. In *Language Interpretation and Communication*, ed. D. Gerver, and H.W. Sinaiko. New York: Plenum Press.

Rinne, R., J. Kivirauma, and H. Simola. 2002. Shoots of revisionist policy or just slow readjustment? The Finnish case of educational reconstruction. *Journal of Education Policy* 17: 643–58.

Robertson, R. 1995. Glocalization: Time-space and homogeneity-heterogeneity. In *Global modernities*, ed. M. Featherstone, S. Lash, and R. Robertson, 25–44. London: Sage.

Summers, M., and C. Kruger. 1994. A longitudinal study of a constructivist approach to improving primary teachers' subject matter knowledge in science. *Teaching and Teacher Education* 10: 499–519.

Taylor, S., F. Rizvi, B. Lingard, and M. Henry. 1997. *Educational policy and the politics of change.* London: Routledge.

Troman, G., and B. Jeffrey. 2005. Providing a framework for a 'shared repertoire' in a cross-national research project. *Methodological Issues and Practices in Ethnography, Studies in Educational Ethnography* 11: 207–25.

Troman, G., and B. Jeffrey. 2007. Qualitative data analysis in cross-cultural projects. *Comparative Education* 43, no. 4: 511–25.

Välijärvi, J., P. Kupari, P. Linnakylä, P. Reinikainen, S. Sulkunen, J. Törnroos, and I. Arffman. 2007. *The Finnish success in PISA – and some reasons behind it 2.* Jyväskylä: Institute for Educational Research.

Vulliamy, G., E. Kimonen, R. Nevalainen, and R. Webb. 1997. Teacher identity and curriculum change: A comparative case-study analysis of small schools in England and Finland. *Comparative Education* 33, no. 1: 97–115.

Vulliamy, G., K. Lewin, and D. Stephens. 1990. *Doing educational research in developing countries: qualitative strategies.* London: Falmer.

Webb, R., K. Häkkinen, S. Hämäläinen, and G. Vulliamy. 1998. External inspection or school self-evaluation? A comparative analysis of policy and practice in primary schools in England and Finland. *British Educational Research Journal* 24, no. 5: 539–56.

Webb, R., and G. Vulliamy. 1996. *Roles and responsibilities in the primary school, changing demands, changing practices.* Buckingham: Open University Press.

Webb, R., and G. Vulliamy. 1999a. Changing times, changing demands: A comparative analysis of classroom practice in primary schools in England and Finland. *Research Papers in Education* 14, no. 3: 229–55.

Webb, R., and G. Vulliamy. 1999b. Managing curriculum policy changes: A comparative analysis of primary schools in England and Finland. *Journal of Education Policy* 14, no. 2: 117–37.

Webb, R., and G. Vulliamy. 2006. *Coming full circle? The impact of New Labour's education policies on primary school teachers' work.* London: ATL.

Webb, R., and G. Vulliamy. Forthcoming. *On a treadmill but the kids are great: Primary teachers' work and well-being.* London: ATL.

Webb, R., G. Vulliamy, S. Hämäläinen, A. Sarja, E. Kimonen, and R. Nevalainen. 2004a. A comparative analysis of primary teacher professionalism in England and Finland. *Comparative Education* 40, no. 1: 83–107.

Webb, R., G. Vulliamy, S. Hämäläinen, A. Sarja, E. Kimonen, and R. Nevalainen. 2004b. Pressures, rewards and teacher retention: A comparative study of primary teaching in England and Finland. *Scandinavian Journal of Educational Research* 48, no. 2: 169–88.

Webb, R., G. Vulliamy, A. Sarja, and S. Hämäläinen. 2006. Globalization and leadership and management: A comparative analysis of primary schools in England and Finland. *Research Papers in Education* 21, no. 4: 407–32.

Welmond, M. 2002. Globalization viewed from the periphery: The dynamics of teacher identity in the republic of Benin. *Comparative Education Review* 46: 37–65.

Woods, P., B. Jeffrey, G. Troman, and M. Boyle. 1997. *Restructuring schools, reconstructing teachers*. Buckingham: Open University Press.

INDEX

Page numbers in *Italics* represent tables.
Page numbers in **Bold** represent figures.

An environmentally friendly book printed and bound in England by www.printondemand-worldwide.com

PEFC Certified

This product is
from sustainably
managed forests
and controlled
sources

www.pefc.org

PEFC/16-33-415

MIX
Paper from
responsible sources
FSC® C004959

FSC
www.fsc.org

This book is made entirely of chain-of-custody materials

#0326 - 180512 - C0 - 246/174/6 - PB